Crossing Over

Jay Rice

Copyright ©2024 by Jay Rice All rights reserved. This book is protected by the copyright laws of the United States of America. This book may not be copied or reprinted for commercial gain or profit. The use of short quotations or occasional page copying for personal or group study is encouraged. Permission will be granted upon request from Jay Rice. All rights reserved. Any emphasis added to Scripture quotations is the author's own.

All quotations are from the New King James Version of the Bible and King James Version of the Bible, unless otherwise noted.
ISBN: 979-8-218-46766-1

TABLE OF CONTENTS

FOREWORD - 1

ACKNOWLEDGEMENTS - 3

INTRODUCTION – 4

KNOW YOUR ENEMY – 10

HOW THE CHURCH LEFT ITS HEBRAIC ROOTS – 34

CROSSING OVER – 43

GO TO THE ROOT TO FIND THE FRUIT – 69

THE WORD BECAME FLESH – 91

APPENDIX - 125

Foreword

It has been said by many scholars, "Judaism doesn't need Christianity to explain it, but Christianity cannot be explained apart from Judaism." That statement is not only correct, it is indisputable.

In Christianity you basically have a new interpretation of Judaism that results in a new way of life. It was established by a Jewish Rabbi named Yeshua. He was able to establish this new way of life because He wasn't just some ordinary Rabbi, He was a Rabbi with *semikhah* (authority).

Most of the Church doesn't realize that Yeshua was a Rabbi. They think He was a carpenter. The reality is, He was not a carpenter but He was a Rabbi. That's why they called Him Rabbi. Just ask yourself a couple questions: Could a carpenter stand in a Synagogue and pick up a scroll and preach? Could a carpenter walk into the Temple and teach? The answer is NO! The reason you do not find Yeshua in the Bible between ages twelve and thirty is because He was in Rabbinical school. At age thirty He comes on the scene and is baptized by John the Baptist. That was His ordination as a Rabbi. At His Baptism two miracles occur. The Father speaks from Heaven and the Holy Spirit sits on Him in the form of a dove. These two miracles give him a status that only happens about once or twice every one hundred years. These two miracles give him *semikhah* or authority. This means He is the most powerful man alive in Israel. Having *semikhah* (authority) means He is the only man alive that can change the interpretation of the Torah. And change it He did!

Yeshua removed the legalism of the Torah and turned Judaism into relationship based worship. He changed Judaism from being a self focused religion into a Kingdom lifestyle.

At the end of the day, Christianity is simply an extension of Judaism. Most of the early believers were Hebrew people who acknowledged Yeshua as the Messiah. They never stopped observing their Hebrew roots. They added the worship of Yeshua to who they already were, therefore becoming complete in the Abrahamic Covenant. As a Gentile you have been grafted into this Covenant. You have been made a citizen of God's Kingdom through the blood of His Son.

Most Gentile believers have been indoctrinated by a Western Church Theology, a Hellenistic mindset. Therefore the idea that God is Himself a Jew and His Son is a Jewish Rabbi is a foreign concept. But true nonetheless. It is impossible to fully grasp the whole truth of Scripture apart from the Hebraic interpretation of the Bible, even the New Testament. God did not write two Bibles. There are not two religions, Judaism and Christianity. There is One God who has One Son and He is the Messiah and King of us all.

In his book _Crossing Over_, Jay Rice does an outstanding job explaining how Gentile believers are an extension of a Hebrew Covenant. His book is an outstanding explanation of how ALL scripture refers back to the Torah and is a fulfillment of the Prophets.

I have been a student of the word for almost forty years. I have earned four Biblical degrees from Universities and Seminaries. I say that not to brag but to emphasize the fact that I learned many truths from Jay's book that I personally did not know. I have been a Hebrew roots teacher for two decades and Jay's book has taught me many truths that I have now added to my Hebraic understanding of Scripture.

As you read this scholarly work, you will be instructed and inspired by the deep and yet practical truths that Jay has laid out for you. Get ready! You are about to embark upon a journey like none you've ever experienced before. However, beware! Many things you have believed to be true will be challenged by the truths contained within this book. If you keep an open mind, you will be much better for the changes that will be made to your understanding of the Word of God.

Dr. Dwain Miller
Senior Pastor, The Edge Church, Cabot AR

ACKNOWLEDGEMENTS

    First and foremost I want to thank God for giving me the opportunity to share the information that is in this book. What I figured would be a local teaching within our community, God intended for the world! Next I want to thank my wife and son. They have both been instrumental and encouraging. To my mom, she has been my biggest cheerleader and I wouldn't be where I am spiritually if it wasn't for her. To my dad for being an encouragement and helping with feedback.

    Pastor John Cates, I thank you for helping me to get started in ministry. Pastor Terry Newman, thank you for introducing me to the Hebraic side of God. Dr. Ron Moseley, I appreciate our meetings and conversations, always insightful! Dr. Scott Stewart, thank you for being one of my main guides on this journey with God and going deeper with the Hebraic root! Pastor Lee Brown, thank you for not just being a Pastor after God's heart, but being a friend as well!

    To Bethany Steele, thank you for painting my cover. You are truly talented. Dave Johnson, thank you for the graphics that you helped create. To Dr. John Philebaum, thanks for the assistance with editing, it's been an honor working with you on this book. Your insight helped a lot. To everyone who helped with feedback, proofing and encouragement, your assistance was so helpful and very much needed.

INTRODUCTION

What you believe to be true, is it true? Or do you believe that it's true because you were taught that it's true & never looked any further? In other words, have you ever questioned the truth you hold? Is it a truth you've discovered or one you've been taught? Have you ever delved deeper to truly understand beyond what you've been told?

Paul said in **1 Corinthians 11:1** "Imitate me, just as I also *imitate* Christ." Paul is saying, imitate me as I imitate Christ. How well do you imitate Paul? Meaning how much do you do what Paul did? For instance, if you had to, could you lead someone to Jesus using only the Tanakh (Old Testament)? If not, why not? When Paul was alive, all that existed was the Tanakh (Old Testament).

These questions are designed to challenge your beliefs and encourage critical thinking. As you progress through this book, they will guide you to a deeper understanding of your faith. **Acts 17:11** "These were more fair-minded than those in Thessalonica, in that they received the word with all readiness, and searched the Scriptures daily *to find out* whether these things were so."

This verse speaks of the people in Berea. They were willing to listen with all readiness of mind, but they searched out what was being said to make sure it was true. In other words, please don't take my word regarding the information shared with you through this book. Search it out for yourself. The problem in society today is that people are taught what to think and not how to think.

Let's demystify Apologetics. It's a word that can evoke different reactions. For some, it's a complex term. For others, it's easily confused with an apology. But for a few, it's a powerful concept that ignites a passion for understanding and defending their beliefs.

So, what exactly is Apologetics? It's quite simply defined - a rational defense of the Christian faith. The word derives from the Greek word **(Apologia)**, meaning a formal defense of a position. Always be ready to give an answer as to why you believe what you do! In other words, don't take my word for anything. Therefore, I challenge you to explore everything I'm going to share with you for yourself and do your own due diligence.

1 Peter 3:15 says, "But sanctify the Lord God in your hearts, and always *be* ready to **give a defense (Apologia)** to everyone who asks you a reason for the hope that is in you, with meekness and fear;"

1 Thessalonians 5:21 Test all things; hold fast what is good.

We're all on different spiritual levels with God. **Ezekiel 47** speaks of a river in which Ezekiel was on the bank or edge of the water. He was then led out into the water, which was ankle-deep, knee-deep, waist-deep, and eventually so deep that he was swimming.

The analogy of this river can represent how deep we choose to go with God! Some people may stand along the shoreline, while others stick their feet in the water. Some people get in a boat and choose to stay in the boat, while others in the boat may run their fingers through the water, and some may stick their feet in the water. Some choose to wade in the water, and some choose to go swimming.

Middle East scholar Kenneth Bailey, has an interesting analogy! "Suppose I've spent my life going to a beach. I've seen waves splashing against rocks, ships on the water, fishermen casting lines. One day at this beach someone says, 'Ken, I have two snorkels. Let's go.'

"Suddenly I see coral, seaweed, and fish. These undersea views in no way invalidate the beauty of what's above. In my work, I'm looking for the coral and the fish."[1]

Bailey states, "These undersea views in no way invalidate the beauty of what's above." A whole other world exists beneath the water, and it's beautiful! We can't necessarily see it on land or in a boat, but it exists! The Bible is like this in many regards. There is much that is seen. However,

---

[1] (https://worship.calvin.edu/resources/resource-library/kenneth-e-bailey-on-jesus-through-middle-eastern-eyes/)

there is much that is not seen. These things that aren't seen are not necessarily hidden because God hid them from us. God wants these things seen. Sometimes, it just takes some treasure hunting. I want to take you for a swim. However, we aren't going on an ordinary swim. We are going diving for treasure! It will be an adventure from the milk of the word to the meat of the word!

Psalms 37:4 tells us that if we delight ourselves in the LORD, He will give us the desires of our hearts.

My desire was that God show me things concerning Himself, Jesus, and the Bible that the average Christian does not necessarily see. God has definitely delivered. He has granted me that desire and helped me write this book so that I can help you who are reading it!

To truly understand the Word of God the way that He intended, there are four ways we must study the Bible:

1. **Linguistically**
The Old Testament was written in Hebrew, except for a few verses in Aramaic, and the New Testament was written in Greek. Even though the New Testament is written in Greek, it is Hebrew text in Greek dress, meaning it is full of Hebraisms.

2. **Culturally**
Looking at the Bible in its Hebraic cultural setting makes things much clearer, instead of looking at it through a Western cultural mindset.

3. **Historically**
Looking at history and how God presents it is exciting and highly informative. As a matter of fact, God even commands us to study history.

Job 8:8-10 "For inquire, please, of the former age, And consider the things discovered by their fathers; For we *were born* yesterday, and know nothing, Because our days on earth *are* a shadow. Will they not teach you and tell you, And utter words from their heart?"

Isaiah 46:9-10 "Remember the former things of old, For I *am* God, and *there is* no other; *I am* God, and *there is* none like Me, Declaring the end from the beginning, And from ancient times *things* that are not *yet* done, Saying, 'My counsel shall stand, And I will do all My pleasure"

Hebrews 10:32 "But recall the former days in which, after you were illuminated, you endured a great struggle with sufferings:"

2 Peter 3:1-2 "Beloved, I now write to you this second epistle (in *both of* which I stir up your pure minds by way of reminder), that you may be mindful of the words which were spoken before by the holy prophets, and of the commandment of us, the apostles of the Lord and Savior"

But why would God want us to know history? The Apostle Paul answers this question in **Romans 15:4.**

Romans 15:4 "For whatever things were written before were written for our learning, that we through the patience and comfort of the Scriptures might have hope."

Judges 2:10 "When all that generation had been gathered to their fathers, another generation arose after them who did not know the LORD nor the work which He had done for Israel."

It only took one generation to forget what God had done for them. Likewise there's been a culmination over approximately the last 1,900 years of Satan using his devices of removing God's Hebraic nature from the church.

4. Geographically

Where do the events of the Bible take place? For the most part, the Bible takes place in Israel and the Middle East.

With that being said, it's important to realize that every time we open the Bible, we are transported back in time, to a different language, a different culture, in a different land. It's also essential to never interpret Scripture from a Western cultural mindset.

Mainstream Christianity, for the most part, has pretty much abandoned its Hebraic roots, and because of that, the Church, by and large, is only seeing Jesus through a Western (Greek) mindset. In doing so, the Church has disabled itself by not being able to see Jesus the way God intended. The point I'm trying to make is that there is more, much more!

This book is by no means meant to be an exhaustive study. However, it is intended to show you the importance of our Hebraic roots and how these Hebraic roots point to Jesus. I'm convinced that once you see the information in this book, you will develop an even more intimate relationship with Jesus and a desire to go deeper! Because honestly once you see these things, you can't unsee them!

We will explore how Satan has used his devices against humanity, as well as show how Satan has weaponized the Church against itself by using replacement theology. One of the issues that we need to address is an identity crisis issue. Many Christians don't know who they are or where they came from. We will learn how, even though Gentiles are grafted in with Jews, Gentiles don't become Jews, but Gentiles become Hebrews along with the Jews.

So what is Hebrew, and why does it matter? Hebrew is one of the languages of the world, but it's not just any language; it's the language of God Himself. However, it is much more than that. Hebrew is, in essence,

God's character, nature, culture, and identity. Hebrew is the root, which is rooted in Jesus. Therefore, we will see not only how Hebrew was, in fact, the language that Jesus primarily spoke but also how Jesus Himself is Hebrew! As Pastor Scott Stewart says, "When you go to the root, you find the fruit!"

So you might be saying to yourself, this sounds like it's just a Jewish thing. Why bother? I'm here to tell you it's not a Jewish thing; it's a God thing, and many have missed what I want to show you!

Ecclesiastes 1:9 tells us that there is nothing new under the sun. With that being said, the information that I have to share is no secret revelation; there is no special sauce or secret formula! It's all been there for us the entire time. However, God has shown me that much has been hidden, lost, or forgotten. Some of you reading this book will see God, Jesus, and the Bible on a much deeper level.

What has humbled me is that I've realized that much of what God has shown me concerning Himself has not been seen by the average Christian over the last 2,000 years! In the words of Pastor Chris Truby, much of the Church has been living off of crumbs while God wants to have a feast! There is so much more!

In reality, much of what is in this book should be basic knowledge for all who have accepted Jesus as their personal Lord and Savior. So why isn't it? The truth is that we have all been robbed! One of the most humbling experiences has been realizing that the more I learn, the more I realize that I don't know. You see, sometimes we have to unlearn so we can learn!

For example, many churches are so focused on salvation that as soon as salvation occurs, it's like another notch has been added, like a trophy for the church and/or Pastor. The person seemingly gets thrown by the wayside, and no discipleship takes place. They seem to forget what Jesus said.

Matthew 28:18 – 20: "And Jesus came and spoke to them, saying, "All authority has been given to Me in heaven and on earth. Go therefore and make disciples of all the nations, baptizing them in the name of the Father and of the Son and of the Holy Spirit, teaching them to observe all things that I have commanded you; and lo, I am with you always, *even* to the end of the age." Amen. Indeed, salvation is important. However, Jesus said before his ascension to go into the world & make disciples.

My new desire is for those reading this book to realize that there's much more with God than we could ever imagine. For you to fully comprehend and understand what God wants me to share with you, I'm going to build a foundation to help you. Please take your time reading this book and glean what you can from God. You don't have to be in a hurry to get through it! Just imagine easing yourself into the water, going deeper and deeper. My goal is for you to develop a more intimate relationship and knowledge of who Jesus is and who you are through Him.

Here is a list of what I call Treasure Hunt verses. I recommend you pray these verses to God, as I have done, and He will show you incredible things!

Jeremiah 29:13 "And you will seek Me and find *Me,* when you search for Me with all your heart."

Jeremiah 33:3 "Call to Me, and I will answer you, and show you great and mighty things, which you do not know."

Psalms 51:6 "Behold, You desire truth in the inward parts, And in the hidden *part* You will make me to know wisdom."

Psalms 25:5 "Lead me in Your truth and teach me, For You *are* the God of my salvation; On You I wait all the day."

Psalms 25:14 "The secret of the LORD *is* with those who fear Him, And He will show them His covenant."

Deuteronomy 29:29 "The secret *things belong* to the LORD our God, but those *things which are* revealed *belong* to us and to our children forever, that *we* may do all the words of this law."

Daniel 2:22 "He reveals deep and secret things; He knows what *is* in the darkness, And light dwells with Him."

Daniel 2:28 "But there is a God in heaven who reveals secrets, and He has made known to King Nebuchadnezzar what will be in the latter days. Your dream, and the visions of your head upon your bed, were these:"

Isaiah 45:3 "I will give you the treasures of darkness And hidden riches of secret places, That you may know that I, the LORD, Who call *you* by your name, *Am* the God of Israel."

Matthew 13:44 "Again, the kingdom of heaven is like treasure hidden in a field, which a man found and hid; and for joy over it he goes and sells all that he has and buys that field."

Psalms 119:18 "Open my eyes, that I may see Wondrous things from Your law."

Psalms 119:130 "The entrance of Your words gives light; It gives understanding to the simple."

Psalms 119:162 "I rejoice at Your word As one who finds great treasure."

Proverbs 25:2 "*It is* the glory of God to conceal a matter, But the glory of kings *is* to search out a matter."

It's like the ultimate game of hide-and-seek—God literally hides things for us to find!

KNOW YOUR ENEMY

People have often said, "What you don't know won't hurt you." We all know that is incorrect, yet many people have adopted this philosophy from the normal routine of their daily lives, especially toward spiritual matters. Nothing could be further from the truth! **Hosea 4:6** says, "My people are destroyed for lack of knowledge." Spiritual ignorance is a very serious matter.

Too often, we equate ignorance with one who is simple-minded or backward. But some of the most talented people in the world, some of the greatest minds in science, are spiritually ignorant. Spiritual ignorance is a greater deficiency than someone who may be intellectually slow.

Spiritual ignorance is not just a condition suffered by those who have not accepted Jesus Christ as their personal Lord and Savior. Unfortunately, it is also true of many who claim to be Christians, including many who are involved in ministry. Have you ever asked yourself, how can a Christian behave this way or that way? The problem is that half of those who are ignorant choose to be ignorant, and the other half don't even realize they're ignorant. This results in a Christian life that is stunted in its growth.

According to the Merriam-Webster dictionary, the definition of "ignorance" is a lack of knowledge, understanding, or education: the state of being ignorant.

"It's easier to fool people than to convince them they have been fooled" – Mark Twain.

A.W. Tozer said, "Satan's greatest weapon is man's ignorance of God's word."

We are familiar with the fact that Satan is known as a deceiver. He wants to kill, steal, and destroy. More often than not, we as believers tend to focus only on those who have been and continue to be deceived outside the body of Christ. I'm referring to those who haven't accepted Jesus as their Lord and Savior. But what about those who have accepted Jesus as their Messiah? Many believers in Messiah, including many pastors, teachers, evangelists, colleges, and seminaries, have been deceived and don't even realize it.

Believe it or not, Satan is a master theologian. His goal is total destruction of us who are made in the image of God. You see, Satan cannot destroy the Word of God, so instead, he lies about it and twists scripture.

Have you ever heard the expression that if you hear something repeated enough, then you will believe it? This is known as the "Illusory Truth Effect". The illusory truth effect describes how, when we are repeatedly exposed to misinformation, we are more likely to believe that it's true. In other words, it is an illusion of the truth!

Adolf Hitler was notorious for using this method against the Jews as well as the world. Hitler said in Mein Kampf, "Such being the case, all effective propaganda must be confined to a few bare essentials, and those must be expressed as far as possible in stereotyped formulas. These slogans should be persistently repeated until the very last individual has come to grasp the idea that has been put forward."[2]

One example of Hitler's use of the illusory truth effect was Theresienstadt. Theresienstadt was one of the concentration camps used by the Nazis during World War II. However, this was no ordinary concentration camp.

Initially, Theresienstadt was created as a minor military base by Austrian Emperor Josef II in 1784 C.E., naming it after his mother, Empress Maria Theresa. It served as a military base for the Habsburg Monarchy until 1918 and then for the First Czechoslovak Republic until 1938. In 1939, the Nazis used the town as a military base until the end of summer 1941. In the fall of 1941, Theresienstadt was converted into a transit camp ghetto. Meaning that Jews would arrive at Theresienstadt and then eventually be hauled away on trains to other concentration camps, like Auschwitz, to be slaughtered.

Theresienstadt was called a spa town for the Jews who were celebrities, elderly, and disabled war vets from World War I who met at least one of two criteria: severely disabled due to war wounds and/or veterans awarded the Iron Cross 1st Class and above. Benito Mussolini, who founded and led the National Fascist Party (PNF), described Theresienstadt as a ghetto where the elderly could draw their pensions and benefits, living their lives out according to their own wishes. However, this was an illusion!

---

[2] Hitler, Adolf. Mein Kampf (Deluxe Hardbound Edition) (p. 243). Sachin Garg. Kindle Edition.

In reality, Theresienstadt was far from the lavish retirement community that the Nazis had portrayed it to be. Once the Jews arrived, they were stripped of their belongings, and many of them were tricked into deeding out their properties, including life insurance policies, in exchange for upscale living conditions that did not exist. There was a Jewish Council of Elders, which consisted of Jewish prisoners at Theresienstadt, who were forced to pick and choose which of their fellow Jews would be deported to killing centers.

Growing concern from Danish leaders and others around the world about what was happening to the Jews by the Nazis began to take shape. In June 1944, the Nazis allowed the Danish Red Cross and the International Red Cross to visit Theresienstadt to see for themselves how good the Jews had it made in the spa town. You're probably thinking, how in the world could the Nazis pull that off?

Elaborate measures were taken to disguise conditions in the ghetto and to portray an atmosphere of normalcy. The SS engaged the Council of Jewish Elders and the camp-ghetto "residents" in a "beautification" program. Prisoners planted gardens, painted housing complexes, renovated barracks, and developed and practiced cultural programs for the entertainment of the visiting dignitaries to convince them that the "Seniors' Settlement" was real. The SS authorities intensified deportations of Jews from the ghetto to alleviate overcrowding. As part of the preparations in the camp ghetto, 7,503 people were deported to Auschwitz between May 16 and May 18, 1944.[3]

When The Red Cross visited, they saw the Jews in Theresienstadt wearing nice clothes, playing in the newly renovated park, and eating decent food. The Red Cross had bought the hoax. The Nazis decided to push their luck even further and created a propaganda film called Theresienstadt. This film was to show the fake living conditions of Theresienstadt, just as the Red Cross had observed, directed by one of the Jewish prisoners by the name of Kurt Gerron. Gerron was a famous Jewish actor and film director involved in many films from 1920 to 1937. After finishing the film, Kurt Gerron was deported to Auschwitz, where he was executed upon arrival.

Of the 140,000 Jews who arrived at Theresienstadt, the Nazis deported nearly 90,000 of them to other concentration camps, where many of them met their doom. At one point, the death rate at Theresienstadt was so high, mostly from disease and starvation, that the Nazis built a crematorium capable of disposing of 200 bodies a day.

---

[3] https://encyclopedia.ushmm.org/content/en/article/theresienstadt-red-cross-visit?series=5

Satan has utilized the illusory truth effect as part of his devices against the Bible. Not only is Satan a theologian and a deceiver, but he is also a master counterfeiter.

Knowing that Satan is enemy number one and his primary goal is to steal, kill, and destroy, it's important to understand the tactics that are being used by our enemy. The Bible tells us in **Ephesians 6:11** "Put on the whole armor of God, that you may be able to stand against the **wiles** of the devil." The word "**wiles**" is what I want to draw your attention to. The word "**wiles**" (methodos) is often translated to carry the idea of something that is cunning, crafty, subtle, or full of trickery. However, the most basic translation of this word is its literal meaning, with a road.[4]

By electing to use this word methodos, Paul tells us how the devil puts his cunning, crafty, subtle, and tricky deception to work. The word "wiles" clearly reveals that the devil operates with a road or on a road.[5]

In **Second Corinthians 2:11**, Paul gives us a clue as to where this road leads that the devil is traveling on. Paul says, "...We are not ignorant of his [Satan's] **devices**."

The word "**devices**" is taken from the word noemata, which is derived from the word nous. The word nous is the Greek word for the mind or the intellect. However, the form noemata, as used by Paul in **Second Corinthians 2:11**, carries the idea of a deceived mind. Specifically, the word noemata denotes Satan's insidious and malevolent plot to fill the human mind with confusion.

The word "**devices**" (noemata) depicts the insidious plots and wicked schemes of Satan to attack and victimize the human mind. One expositor has even stated that the word "**devices**" bears the notion of mind games. With this in mind, you could translate the verse, "...We are not ignorant of the mind games that Satan tries to pull on us."[6]

Why would Satan want to attack your mind? Your mind is the part of the image of God where God communicates with you and reveals His will to you. God renews our lives by renewing our minds, and he renews

---

[4] Renner, Rick. Dressed to Kill: A Biblical Approach to Spiritual Warfare and Armor (p. 172). Harrison House Publishers. Kindle Edition.

[5] Renner, Rick. Dressed to Kill: A Biblical Approach to Spiritual Warfare and Armor (p. 172). Harrison House Publishers. Kindle Edition.

[6] Renner, Rick. Dressed to Kill: A Biblical Approach to Spiritual Warfare and Armor (pp. 173-174). Harrison House Publishers. Kindle Edition.

our minds through his truth.[7]

So, it's fair to say that Satan's tactics revolve around deception and lies. Jesus calls Satan the father of lies. **John 8:44** "You are of *your* father the devil, and the desires of your father you want to do. He was a murderer from the beginning, and does not stand in the truth, because there is no truth in him. When he speaks a lie, he speaks from his own *resources,* for he is a liar and the father of it."

Remember the seemingly harmless question the subtle serpent asked Eve in the garden? **Genesis 3:1** "Has God indeed said…?" So slight, so simple, yet so deadly! Satan often disguises things not necessarily to appear evil or sinful but to appear innocent. In fact, it can even appear to be good or even pleasant. The subtle temptation of Genesis reveals Satan's clever "good and pleasant" message.

Genesis 3:6 "So when the woman saw that the tree *was* good for food, that it *was* pleasant to the eyes, and a tree desirable to make *one* wise, she took of its fruit and ate. She also gave to her husband with her, and he ate."

As Eve saw the forbidden fruit, it was good and it was pleasant. Yet it was deadly! The Bible says in **2 Corinthians 11:14**, "And no marvel; for Satan himself is transformed into an angel of light." He tries mimicking God as closely as he can. A better picture of the Devil might have been a good-looking young man in a black suit with a clerical collar. Satan loves religion. He closely imitates the truth, but he cannot be trusted because, by his very nature, he is an impostor—a counterfeit, a teller of deliberate falsehoods.[8]

It's staggering to think that the average Christian only studies the Word of God 7 minutes a month, which equates to 94 minutes a year, which is just barely over an hour and a half a year! The average Christian only hears about 48 hours of the Word a year from Church! Only 37% of Pastors hold a Biblical worldview! Because of this, many have fallen victim to and continue to be ignorant of Satan's deceptions and counterfeits. Much of it seems so subtle and harmless. However, I'm going to show you a progression so you can see just how dangerous and destructive it can be.

Satan's Counterfeits

"There is no neutral ground in the universe; every square inch, every split second, is claimed by God and counterclaimed by Satan" C.S. Lewis

---

[7] Miller, Dwain. Jesus the Rabbi: Unlocking the Hebraic Teaching of Yeshua (p. 137). Kindle Edition.

[8] Cross, John R.. The Stranger on the Road to Emmaus: Who was the Man? What was the Message? (pp. 97-98). GoodSeed International. Kindle Edition.

God presents Himself as the Holy Trinity Father, Son, and Spirit - Satan presents as the unholy trinity: Beast, Dragon, and False Prophet (**Revelation 12-13**).

God blesses the earth with signs, wonders and miracles - Satan causes "lying signs wonders and miracles" (**2 Thessalonians 2:9**).

God sends the Messiah to save our souls - Satan sends false Messiahs to deceive our souls. (**Matthew. 24:23**).

God sends prophets to declare His message to the nations - Satan sends false prophets to poison the well of faith. (**Matthew 7:15**).

We went from Evening to Morning, to Morning to Evening – The Bible tells us that days begin in the evening (**Genesis 1:5**)

God's calendar to Gregorian calendar – We went from a lunar calendar to a solar calendar (Initiated by Pope Gregory in 1582)

We went from B.C. (Before Christ) /A.D. (Anno Domini) to B.C.E (Before Common Era) /C.E. (Common Era) - Jesus literally split time in half!

Mazzaroth to Horoscopes – The Mazzaroth is the ecliptic belt of constellations around the earth. In Greek, it is called the Zodiac, which means "The Way". However, Mazzaroth is a Hebrew word meaning "Garland of Crowns." For more than 2,500 years, the world was without a written revelation from God. The question is, did God leave himself without a witness? This question is answered very positively by the written word that He did not. **Psalms 19:1-3** "To the Chief Musician. A Psalm of David. The heavens declare the glory of God; And the firmament shows His handiwork. Day unto day utters speech, And night unto night reveals knowledge. *There is* no speech nor language *Where* their voice is not heard." One aspect of the stars was to tell the story of the Gospel in the constellations by using the original name & meaning of the stars, which is called the Mazzaroth. Satan turned Astronomy, which is "the study of stars" to Astrology, which is "the worship of stars" with horoscopes.

Dinosaurs supposedly lived 65 million years before man – Yet Dinosaurs and man were created on the same day, and death did not exist until man sinned (**Genesis 1:24-31**)

Passover to Easter – We went from celebrating the death, burial & resurrection of Jesus with Passover to celebrating something called Easter, which incorporates a (Gender confused) rabbit who lays eggs that has nothing to do with Jesus. (Initiated by Constantine in 325 C.E. Council of Nicea)

Good Friday to Easter Sunday – Simple math shows that it is not three days & three nights.

Judaism vs. Christianity - Judaism and Christianity are, in essence, one, but they have been pitted against each other as dueling rivals or religions! We will dive deeper into this later.

The terms "Old Testament" and "New Testament" – The Hebrew word for covenant is Brit (ברית). The word covenant is mentioned 282 times in the **Tanakh**, which is the Hebrew word for (Old Testament), otherwise known as the "Hebrew Scriptures" and is the foundation for both Judaism and Christianity. It is more commonly known as the "Old Testament". The word "old" was attached to it to convey that it is basically obsolete or done away with.

TaNaKh – is actually a three-letter acronym.
TNK – TORAH – NEVI'IM – KETUVIM
Torah ("instruction"), Nevi'im ("prophets"), and Ketuvim ("writings").

Covenant Renewed – The word covenant is mentioned 30 times in The New Testament, which in Hebrew is called Brit Chadashah (ברית חדשה), which means **"Covenant Renewed,"** otherwise referred to as the "Apostolic Scriptures" or "Christian Scriptures"!

Jeremiah 31:31 in our English Bible says "Behold, the days are coming, says the LORD, when I will make a <u>new covenant</u> with the house of Israel, and with the house of Judah:"

We know that the book of Jeremiah was originally written in Hebrew. (Please note that I have underlined Brit Chadashah (ברית חדשה), which means **"Covenant Renewed"**). The original Hebrew of **Jeremiah 31:31** reads,

הנה ימים באים נאם־יהוה וכרתי את־בית ישראל ואת־בית יהודה <u>ברית חדשה</u>:

Remember, Hebrew is read from right to left! The Hebrew rendition of **Jeremiah 31:31** reads, "Behold the days are coming say's Yahweh and I will make with the house of Israel and with the house of Judah a <u>covenant renewed</u>."

Likewise, **Hebrews 8:8** repeats **Jeremiah 31:31** "Because finding fault with them, He says: "BEHOLD, THE DAYS ARE COMING, SAYS THE LORD, WHEN I WILL MAKE A <u>**NEW COVENANT**</u> WITH THE HOUSE OF ISRAEL AND WITH THE HOUSE OF JUDAH— "

The original Greek of **Hebrews 8:8** reads, *"μεμφομενος γαρ αυτοις λεγει ιδου ημεραι ερχονται λεγει κυριος και συντελεσω επι τον οικον ισραηλ και επι τον οικον ιουδα <u>διαθηκην καινην</u>"*.

The Greek rendition of **Hebrews 8:8** reads, "Finding fault for with them, He says Behold the days are coming says the Lord and I will ratify with the house of Israel and with the house of Judah a **covenant renewed**."

Among the many new concepts of Western Civilization, none have had a more profound impact on Western thought than the terms "Old Testament" and "New Testament." Simply because it is from these two concepts that the boundaries between the East and West, the Old World and the New World, Judaism and Christianity have been established in the minds and hearts of the peoples of the world.[9]

So, how did we go from covenant to testament? Before the term "testament" was used in the 1611 Authorized King James Version, it was employed in the old Latin Vulgate and continued to be used by Jerome, in 382 C.E., in his revised Latin Vulgate. From that point on Jerome's new Latin Vulgate became the standard Bible used by all Christians for the next 1,000 years. By the time the King James Version was published in 1611, the term "testament" was well-established within the Christian community and, therefore, left in the King James text by English Protestant translators. The problem with the use of the term "testament" is that it does not exist in the best extant Greek manuscripts.[10]

Bible language scholar Dr. E. W. Bullinger writes: The word "Testament," as a translation of the Greek word diatheke (which means 'covenant'), has been nothing less than a great calamity; for, but its use, truth has been effectively veiled all through the centuries; causing a wrong turning to be taken… by which the errors of tradition have usurped the place of important truth. The word "Testament" as a name for a collection of books is unknown to Scripture. It comes to us through the Latin Vulgate. This was the rendering in the older Latin Versions before Jerome's time; but Jerome, while using foedus or practum for the Hebrew berith in the O.T., unfortunately reverted to testamentum in his version of his N.T. translation (A.D. 382-405). Some of the Latin Fathers preferred instrumentum much in

---

[9] Rhoades, Richard N.. Faith of the Ages: The Hebraic Roots of the Christian Faith (p. 61). iUniverse. Kindle Edition.
[10] Rhoades, Richard N.. Faith of the Ages: The Hebraic Roots of the Christian Faith (p. 61). iUniverse. Kindle Edition.

the sense of our legal use of the word. Rufinus uses the expression novum et vetus instrumentum, and Augustine uses both words instrumentum and testamentum. From the Vulgate, the word testament passed both into the English Bibles and the German.[11]

So we hear the terms "old" and "new" as if one outweighs the other. When in reality, they are both one and the same. This is another example of the illusory truth effect! (A more detailed explanation of covenants will be explored later).

Torah vs Law: We see the term **"Law"** quite often in our Bibles, especially in the Brit Chadashah (New Testament). "Law refers to the first five books in the Bible, known as the (תורה) "Torah" in Hebrew and "Pentateuch" in Greek. The English word "Law" comes from the Greek word (νομον) "Nomos." The word **"Law"** is probably one of the most misunderstood concepts in all of Christianity.

For many Christians, the term, **"Law"** produces a negative mental and spiritual image of rules and regulations along with do's and don'ts. The Greek word **"Law" (νομον) "Nomos"** is like being taken to appear before a judge and jury, to hear your sentence and find out which punishment awaits you for the crimes you have committed. This definition resembles punishment after a law has been broken. In the context of "Law" from a Western cultural (American) mindset, God is often imagined as a hardened lawgiver and harsh judge in the courtroom. Along with this mindset, God is viewed as a God of anger and wrath! Unfortunately, this is another example of the illusory truth effect, an illusion of truth!

As stated above, the word **"Law"** comes from the **Hebrew** word (תורת) **"Torah,"** which literally means **teaching or instruction**! That's quite the difference from **"Law" (Nomos)**. **Psalms 119:18** says, "Open thou mine eyes, that I may behold wondrous things out of thy law." If you replace **"Law"** in this verse with its proper meaning or context, it would read **Psalms 119:18** "Open thou mine eyes, that I may behold wondrous things out of thy **(teaching or instruction)**. As you can see, this puts things into a different perspective. **The law refers to the teaching** or **instructions** of God!

---

[11] Companion Bible, "Appendix Notes," by E. W. Bullinger, (Grand Rapids, MI: Kregel Publications, orig. pub. 1922), #95, pp. 137-138.

The Hebrew word for **"Law"** (**תורת**) (Torah) is like being taken to your father's house for a family gathering with your brothers and sisters, to hear your father teach you and give you instructions on how to protect yourself and gain eternal life. This definition resembles preventative measures or training to help you avoid breaking a law in the first place.

Another thing to consider is that sin is often defined as missing the mark. What is the mark? The mark is **Torah**, God's teaching and instructions, which are provided for all of us to protect us, not hold us in bondage!

Law vs Grace: Perhaps you've heard that we are no longer under the law but under grace. **Romans 6:14** "For sin shall not have dominion over you: for ye are not under the law, but under grace." Tragically, this is one of several verses that is taken out of context in an attempt to do away with the **Tanakh (Old Testament)**.

Indeed, we are no longer under the **law of sin & death**! However, grace is not a New Testament concept! Common misunderstandings about Apostle Paul we don't consider is the time in which Paul lived. We have to transfer 21st-century thinking into a first-century mindset. Paul was Torah observant (**Acts 21**) and wrote from a **Hebraic perspective** in the first century.

Secondly, we don't realize that there are different kinds of laws. To fully understand what Paul is saying, we must strive to understand to whom he is writing and which law he is referring: Law of Bondage (**Romans 7:5-7**); Law of Christ (**Galatians 6:2**); Law of God (**Romans 7:22**); Law of Sin & Death (**Romans 6:14, 8:2**); Law of Liberty (**James 1:25**) of the Perfect Law (**James 1:25**).

Consider the fact that the Greek word is usually translated as "grace" in the Apostolic Scriptures (New Testament); Charis occurs 155 times. The word eleos, usually rendered as "mercy," only occurs 27 times. **That totals 182 Times!**

The Hebrew word commonly translated as "grace," chein occurs only 70 times in the Tanach (Old Testament). However, the word chesed, which is rendered as either "mercy" or "lovingkindness," appears 255 times. **That totals 325 times!**

Grace is mentioned more in the Old Testament than in the New Testament. Therefore, grace is not a New Testament concept.

A few examples of grace in the Tanakh (Old Testament):
- **Adam and Eve found grace when God clothed them**
- **Noah and his family found grace from God during the flood**
- **Abraham found grace when God blessed him with Isaac**

- **Moses and the Israelites found grace as God led them through the parted Red Sea**

Also, in the previous section, we learned that **"Law"** means **"teaching"** or **"instruction."** So, if by some chance you are still convinced that we are no longer under God's **"Law,"** then let's take a look at **Romans 6:14; with that particular mindset, however,** using the proper meaning of **"Law"** (**Torah**). "For sin shall not have dominion over you: for ye are not under the **teaching or instructions of God**, but under grace."

Sounds pretty crazy, right? No longer being under the **teaching** or **instruction** of God sounds very dangerous and would be void of grace! Here's **Romans 6:14** in proper context, "For sin shall not have dominion over you: for ye are not under the **instruction of sin and death**, but under grace."

Peter also warns those who have difficulty understanding Paul's letters and who twist Scripture to their own destruction.

2 Peter 3:16-18 "as also in all his epistles, speaking in them of these things, in which are some things hard to understand, which untaught and unstable *people* twist to their own destruction, as *they do* also the rest of the Scriptures. You therefore, beloved, since you know *this* beforehand, beware lest you also fall from your own steadfastness, being led away with the error of the wicked, **but grow in the grace and knowledge of our Lord and Savior Jesus Christ**. To Him *be* the glory both now and forever. Amen."

Notice in verse 18: Peter says to not only grow in grace, but to grow in the knowledge of our Lord and Saviour Jesus Christ. **Jesus said to learn of Himself in Matthew.**

Matthew 11:29 " Take My yoke upon you and **learn from Me**, for I am gentle and lowly in heart, and you will find rest for your souls."

Cherry Pickers Paradise

Another clever tactic that Satan has utilized aside from counterfeiting that goes right along with the "Illusory Truth Effect" is the twisting of certain sayings and phrases that the average Christian and non-Christian alike believe:

Money Is The Root Of All Evil: – Every time I go somewhere to speak & I ask what is the root of all evil, I always have at least one person say money! However, take a look at **1 Timothy 6:10** "For **the love of money** is a root of all *kinds of* evil, for which some have strayed from the faith in their greediness, and pierced themselves through with many sorrows. " As you can see here, the love of money is the root of all evil. Not money itself!

When A Bell Rings An Angel Receives Its Wings: – I know some of you are laughing at this one, But believe it or not, there are some that believe this phrase came from the Bible. Although it sounds nice, this was a famous phrase from one of the greatest Christmas movies of all time: It's a Wonderful Life!

Men Have One Less Rib Than Women: – Yes, the Bible says God took a rib from Adam and created Eve! **Genesis 2:21-22** "And the LORD God caused a deep sleep to fall on Adam, and he slept; and He took one of his ribs, and closed up the flesh in its place. Then the rib which the LORD God had taken from man He made into a woman, and He brought her to the man." There are some who attempt to argue that Man has one less rib than women in trying to defend the Bible. However, it's a proven medical fact that both men & women have the same number of ribs. Therefore, this argument should not be used!

Peter At The Pearly Gates: – I remember being a little kid thinking that Peter would greet me at the entrance of heaven. This idea came from 3 verses. **Matthew 16:18-19** "And I also say to you that you are Peter, and on this rock, I will build My church, and the gates of Hades shall not prevail against it. And I will give you the keys of the kingdom of heaven, and whatever you bind on earth will be bound in heaven, and whatever you loose on earth will be loosed in heaven." **Revelation 21:21** "The twelve gates *were* twelve pearls: each individual gate was of one pearl. And the street of the city *was* pure gold, like transparent glass." Basically, these verses were taken out of context & imaginations ensued. The image from **Matthew 16:8-9** is that Peter holds the keys to the gates & **Revelation 21:21** says the gates are made of pearl!

The Lion Shall Lay Down With The Lamb: – This is one of the most misquoted sayings from the Bible. Isaiah 11:6 comes to mind because it is often misquoted: "And the wolf will dwell with the lamb, and the leopard will lie down with the young goat, and the calf and the young lion and the fatling together..." Similarly, **Isaiah 65:25** reads, "The wolf and the lamb shall feed together, The lion shall eat straw like the ox..." Although this sentiment reads true, hunter and prey will be reconciled and live in peace with one another for eternity. The actual "Lion and the Lamb" passage is **Revelation 5:5-6**. The Lion and the Lamb both refer to Jesus Christ. He is both the conquering Lion of the tribe of Judah and the Lamb who was slain. The Lion and the Lamb are descriptions of two aspects of the nature of Christ. As the Lion of Judah, He fulfills the prophecy of **Genesis 49:9** and is the Messiah who would come from the tribe of Judah. As the Lamb of God, He is the perfect and ultimate sacrifice for sin.

Cleanliness Is Next To Godliness: Although this phrase may sound biblical, it's not found in the Bible. John Wesley first used it in a sermon in 1788.

God Will Never Give You More Than You Can Handle: - At times, we all face trials & tribulations. And during these times when we are being comforted by a loved one, they may say, "God will never give you more than you can handle." This famous saying is not found in the Bible. The misconception comes from **1 Corinthians 10:13** "No temptation has overtaken you except such as is common to man; but God *is* faithful, who will not allow you to be tempted beyond what you are able, but with the temptation will also make the way of escape, that you may be able to bear *it.*"

This verse says that you will not be tempted beyond your ability but that God will always give you a way out.

Spare The Rod, Spoil The Child: - There is often confusion between this phrase and a biblical Proverb regarding "sparing the rod." This phrase was actually coined by a 17th-century poet and satirist by the name of Samuel Butler in his poem "Hudibras." The poem's main characters, Hudibras and the widow he longs for, are planning to start a love affair, but before the widow commits to it, she asks Hudibras to prove his love for her by committing to twisted acts. The widow then states:

"If matrimony and hanging go By dest'ny, why not whipping too? What med'cine else can cure the fits Of lovers when they lose their wits? Love is a boy by poets stil'd; Then, spare the rod and spoil the child."

The verse that is closely related to it is, **Proverbs 13:24** "He who spares his rod hates his son, But he who loves him disciplines him promptly."

In the time scripture was written, and even today, shepherds still use various tools to guide their sheep. They use a staff, a crook, and a rod. The crook is the curved end of the stick at the end of the staff. When sheep fall into a pit or lose sight of their flock, they look down. The curved end of the crook is used to pull the sheep's head back up and guide it in the way it should go. In the same way, the rod is used to guide sheep who begin to splinter away from the flock back together. It can also be used defensively to keep the sheep safe from predators.

It Is Better To Cast Your Seed In The Belly Of A Whore Than Spill It On The Ground: – **Genesis 38:9** is the Scripture associated with this phrase that's taken out of context. **Genesis 38:9** "But Onan knew that the heir would not be his; and it came to pass, when he went in to his brother's wife, that he emitted on the ground, lest he should give an heir to his brother."

David Guzik explains this passage in his commentary:

"When Onan's brother Er died, it was the duty of his unmarried brothers to "marry" Er's wife and to give her sons. The child would be considered the son of the brother who had died, because really the living brother was acting in his place. This was done so that the dead brother's name would be carried on; but also, so that the widow would have children who could support her. Apart from this, she would likely live the rest of her life as a destitute widow. Onan refused to take this responsibility seriously; he was more than happy to use Tamar for his own sexual gratification, but he did not want to give Tamar a son that he would have to support, but would be considered to be the son of Tamar's late husband Er. Onan pursued sex as only a pleasurable experience; if he really didn't want to father a child by Tamar, why did he have sex with her at all? He refused to fulfill his obligation to his dead brother and Tamar. Many Christians have used this passage as a proof-text against masturbation; indeed, masturbation has been called "onanism." However, this does not seem to be the case here; whatever Onan was doing, he was not masturbating! This was not a sin of masturbation, but a sin of refusing to care for his brother's widow by giving her offspring, and of a selfish use of sex."

To Thine Own Self Be True: – This is not in the Bible! It comes from William Shakespeare's Hamlet. Sometimes, folks get confused about Shakespeare's quotes because he used over 2,000 Bible verses in his writings.

God Helps Those Who Help Themselves: – 1 in 8 people believe the Bible says this phrase, but it simply isn't there! The Bible teaches the exact opposite when you look at **Proverbs 28:26** "He who trusts in his own heart is a fool, But whoever walks wisely will be delivered."

Benjamin Franklin popularized this phrase in the 1757 edition of Poor Richard's Almanac. It had first appeared in the Poor Richard's Almanac in 1733. This phrase originates from one of Aesop's tales called "Hercules & the Wagoneer."

A WAGGONEER was once driving a heavy load along a very muddy way. At last he came to a part of the road where the wheels sank half-way into the mire, and the more the horses pulled, the deeper sank the wheels. So the Waggoner threw down his whip, and knelt down and prayed to Hercules the Strong. "O Hercules, help me in this my hour of distress," quoth he. But Hercules appeared to him, and said:

"Tut, man, don't sprawl there. Get up and put your shoulder to the wheel.
"The gods help them that help themselves."

Pride Comes Before The Fall: – The verse being misquoted here is, **Proverbs 16:18** "Pride *goes* before destruction, And a haughty spirit before a fall." This verse implies that pride comes before destruction & an arrogant spirit before a fall!

Jesus Crucified On A Dogwood Tree: - There is a commonly told story that the dogwood tree was chosen as the wood for the cross on which Jesus Christ was crucified.

The Legend of the Dogwood

"When Christ was on earth, the dogwood grew To a towering size with a lovely hue. Its branches were strong and interwoven, And for Christ's cross its timbers were chosen. "Being distressed at the use of the wood, Christ made a promise which still holds good: 'Never again shall the dogwood grow To be large enough for a tree, and so, Slender and twisted it shall always be,

With cross-shaped blossoms for all to see. "'The petals shall have bloodstains marked brown, And in the blossom's center a thorny crown. All who see it will think of me, Nailed to a cross from a dogwood tree. Protected and cherished this tree shall be, A reflection to all of my agony."

The pink dogwood is said to represent the blushing of shame for shedding innocent blood. The weeping dogwood represents a heartfelt cry over this tree's being used to crucify Christ.

God has placed many reminders on earth that should cause us to glorify Him for His wonderful greatness, mercy, and love. Dogwood flowers can do just that.

But we should keep in mind that there is nothing in the Bible about Christ being crucified on a dogwood tree. There is no mention of dogwoods in the Bible, even though the word was in use when the King James Version was produced in AD 1611.

The dogwood legend almost certainly originated in North America—it fits the flowering time, the language, and the American folk myth style.

No reference to the dogwood legend before the 20th century can be found. It appeared in The Victoria Advocate newspaper on Sunday, April 18, 1954 (page 3B), and had a history before this, but there are no ancient records of it.

Dogwoods don't grow in Israel.
To further check an essential detail of this story, the Information Center at the Ministry of Tourism in Israel was contacted to determine whether dogwoods grow in Jerusalem, Israel, or the surrounding areas.

Their reply?

"No, the dogwood doesn't grow naturally in or near Israel. It is native to Europe, eastern Asia, and North America only."

Elijah Taken By A Chariot Of Fire: – If you look at the text, you can see that a whirlwind took Elijah & that the chariot of fire was there to test Elisha. **2 Kings 2:11** "Then it happened, as they continued on and talked, that suddenly a chariot of fire *appeared* with horses of fire, and separated the two of them; and Elijah went up by a whirlwind into heaven."

Delilah Cut Samson's Hair: – Here's another example of a mistold tale! **Judges 16:19** "Then she lulled him to sleep on her knees, and called for a man and had him shave off the seven locks of his head. Then she began to torment him, and his strength left him."
Delilah called for a man to cut Samson's hair!

Hate the sin, love the sinner: – This was a quote from Ghandi in 1929. Also, Augustine in 424 A.D. said, "With love for mankind & hatred of sins."

Blessed & highly favored: – This saying more than likely came from, **Luke 1:28** "And having come in, the angel said to her, "Rejoice, highly favored *one,* the Lord *is* with you; blessed *are* you among women!"

This too shall pass: The phrase was first attributed to King Solomon in non-Jewish sources and used by Abraham Lincoln in one of his speeches.

God moves in mysterious ways: - The closest biblical reference to this is **Isaiah 55:8** "For My thoughts *are* not your thoughts, Nor *are* your ways My ways," says the LORD." However, "Light Shining out of Darkness " is a Christian hymn written in 1773 by William Cowper from England. Has the beginning phrase "God moves in a mysterious way."

Follow your heart: – In fact, the Bible tells us to do the complete opposite. **Jeremiah 17:9** "The heart *is* deceitful above all *things,* And desperately wicked; Who can know it?"

The Apple being the forbidden fruit: – In Genesis chapter 3, we read about Adam & Eve eating fruit from the tree of knowledge of good & evil, however there is no evidence that it was an apple. It could have been an apple, or it could have been a fig since they used fig leaves to cover themselves. Or perhaps they ate a pomegranate, which apparently has 613 seeds in it & which represents the 613 laws found in the (Tanakh), or Old Testament!

Dec 25th: is Jesus birthday: – Careful analysis of the Bible shows that Jesus' birthday was during the Feast of Tabernacles, which occurs in early fall.

3 Wisemen: – The Bible does not say anywhere how many wise men there were. It could have been 20 or more.

The Rope Around The High Priest's Ankle: – Another commonly told story among Christians is that on the Day of Atonement, the high priest would go into the Holy of Holies in the temple to make sacrifices. It was said that he would wear bells on his person and have a rope tied around his ankle. The idea is that if he had failed to thoroughly purify himself of all sin, or if he did the sacrifice wrong, God would kill him on the spot. If that happened, then the other priests would have to pull him out! Dr. W.E. Nunnally, a professor of Hebrew and early Judaism, has reported:

"The rope on the high priest legend is just that: a legend. It has obscure beginnings in the Middle Ages and keeps getting repeated. It cannot be found anywhere in the Bible, the Apocrypha, the Dead Sea Scrolls, Josephus, the Pseudepigrapha, the Talmud, Mishna, or any other Jewish source. It just is not there."

Here's the reference from which this myth originated: "Rabbi Yitzchak said, A chain was tied to the feet of the High Priest, when he entered THE HOLY OF HOLIES, so that if he dies there they will take him out, SINCE IT IS FORBIDDEN TO ENTER THERE… Then there is joy among the higher and lower beings. If not, they were all in sorrow and all knew that their prayer was not accepted."[12]

The Book Of James: - The brother of Jesus is identified in the New

---

[12] Zohar Vol. 16 Emor, Section 34. Yom Kippur, Par. 251.

Testament as "James." His Epistle is known as "the Epistle of James." But what if I told you that's not his name? What if I told you his name was actually Jacob? Jacob derives from the Late Latin "Iacobus" and the Greek "Iakobos". John Wycliffe translated the Bible into English from the Latin Vulgate in the 1300's. When he did so, he translated Jacob into James, and it has stuck ever since!

Six Day Creation: – There are many that have trouble with this one! But it's actually quite simple. **2 Peter 3:8** "But, beloved, do not forget this one thing, that with the Lord one day *is* as a thousand years, and a thousand years as one day." The original Hebrew text not only teaches a six-day creation, but it goes out of its way to do so. The textual construction "And the evening and the morning …" at the end of each creation day ("Yom" in Hebrew) indicates that God wants us to know that these days were just like any normal solar day, divided between night-time and daylight.

The very first time the phrase is used, in **Genesis 1:5**, the Hebrew uses the cardinal number "one" ("echad" in Hebrew). In the following uses of the phrase "…the evening and the morning…", the Hebrew switches to using ordinal numbers – second, third, fourth, fifth, and sixth – referring to each day. It is as if God wishes to clarify that each "yom" consists of day and night. Indeed, what we call a "day" consists of a cycle of day-time and night-time divided into 24 hours. Also, something to consider is that the word "Yom" (Day) is used 2,301 times in the Old Testament but is only questioned in Genesis!

God Did Not Change Saul's Name To Paul: – Contrary to popular belief, God did not change Saul's name to Paul. The myth is that once Saul had his encounter with Jesus on the road to Damascus, Jesus then changed his name to Paul once he converted to Christianity. However, if you notice in Acts chapter 9, there is no mention of his name being changed to Paul. As a matter of fact, he was called Saul until **Acts 13:9**. Saul was his Hebrew name, while Paul was his Greek name. As Paul journeyed farther into the Hellenistic (Greek) world, he was called Paul! **There was no conversion! Paul maintained his Hebrew identity.**

Idioms

An idiom is a figure of speech. It is a word that might mean a particular thing. However, you apply it to something else. For example, in our Western culture, we have sayings such as, "It's raining cats and dogs," "He kicked the bucket," or "She has a silver spoon." All languages have idioms.

The Bible is full of **Hebraic** idioms, and much of the time, when they are translated into English, it can be hard to decipher. However, these idioms can be easily understood once Scripture is contextualized properly. Scripture is most accurately interpreted within its **Hebraic** cultural context. The word "context" comes from the Latin verb "contexere" and means "to weave". A book or any other writing consists of words and thoughts woven together. It is important to understand what the author would have understood regarding Biblical interpretation. Because if you take the text out of context, you're left with a "con"!

Meaning that we can't look at Scripture with a 21st-century mindset. This implies an awareness of the culture that would have affected that understanding. In other words, in order to understand the meaning of words from a different culture, we must understand the culture of the people linguistically, historically, and geographically. Much of our doctrinal differences would be resolved if more people understood the **Hebrew** culture that serves as the background for Scripture. It is important to understand that oftentimes, concerning the Bible, there is a difference in what something says versus what it actually means. That difference is a cultural divide.

Listed below are just a few of the hundreds of idioms found in the Bible!

Healing in His Wings: Malachi 4:2 "But to you who fear My name The Sun of Righteousness shall arise With healing in His **wings**; And you shall go out And grow fat like stall-fed calves."

God commanded the Israelites to place special tassels on the corners of their garments. These tassels, called Tzitzit, represented a symbol of their commitment to obeying God's commandments, found in the Torah.

Numbers 15:37-40 "Again the LORD spoke to Moses, saying, "Speak to the children of Israel: Tell them to make tassels on the **corners** of their garments throughout their generations, and to put a blue thread in the tassels of the **corners**. And you shall have the tassel, that you may look upon it and remember all the commandments of the LORD and do them, and that you *may* not follow the harlotry to which your own heart and your own eyes are inclined, and that you may remember and do all My commandments, and be holy for your God."

The Torah contains 613 commandments or precepts. These include positive commandments to perform an act and negative commandments to abstain from certain acts. The negative commandments number 365, which coincides with the number of days in the solar year, and the positive commandments number 248, which is said to be the number of bones and main organs in the human body.[13]

---

[13] Babylonian Talmud, *Makkot* 23b–24a

"Tallit" is the **Hebrew** word for the "Prayer Shawl," and the "Tzitzit" is the Hebrew word for the corners of the "Prayer Shawl." The number of "Tzitzit" or knotted fringes of the tallit or prayer shawl worn by pious Jews at prayer is connected to the 613 commandments: the **Hebrew** numerical value of the word "Tzitzit" is 600; each tassel has eight threads (when doubled over) and five sets of knots, totaling 13; the sum of these numbers is 613. This reflects the idea that donning a tallit or prayer shawl with "Tzitzit" reminds its wearer of all 613 Torah commandments.

It's important to understand where the "Tzitzit" are attached. The **Hebrew** word for **wings** is (כָּנָף) "kanaf," and it refers to the corner of a tallit or prayer shawl. The ancients taught that the coming Messiah would have special healing powers in the Tzitzit attached to the **corner** of his robe.

Matthew 9:18-22 "While He spoke these things to them, behold, a ruler came and worshiped Him, saying, "My daughter has just died, but come and lay Your hand on her and she will live." So Jesus arose and followed him, and so *did* His disciples. And suddenly, a woman who had a flow of blood for twelve years came from behind and touched the **hem** of His garment. For she said to herself, "If only I may touch His garment, I shall be made well." But Jesus turned around, and when He saw her He said, "Be of good cheer, daughter; your faith has made you well." And the woman was made well from that hour."

When a woman who had been suffering from bleeding for more than twelve years grabbed the **hem**, or **corner** of Jesus' garment, she was showing that she believed Jesus was the expected Messiah and that He could heal her. But she was also declaring that Jesus fulfilled the prophecy of the Sun of Righteousness with healing in his **wings** in **Micah 4:2**.

Jesus also displays this example of healing in His wings in **Matthew 14:34-36** "When they had crossed over, they came to the land of Gennesaret. And when the men of that place recognized Him, they sent out into all that surrounding region, brought to Him all who were sick, and begged Him that they might only touch the **hem** of His garment. And as many as touched *it* were made perfectly well."

John the Baptist eating Locust: Matthew 3:4 "Now John himself was clothed in camel's hair, with a leather belt around his waist; and his food was locusts and wild honey."

In our English language and culture, we hear the word "locust" and automatically associate it with a bug or grasshopper. However, in Israeli culture, the Carob pods from the Carob tree are called "locusts." The Carob tree (Ceratonia siliqua) is native to the eastern Mediterranean region, where it grows naturally. The tree grows to around 50 ft. (15 m) tall and has glossy leaves with thick leaflets. Its red flowers are followed by flat, leathery pods that contain 5-15 hard brown beans embedded in a sweet, edible pulp that tastes like chocolate! Another interesting note is that the Carob pods are also known as St. John's bread! Even to this very day in Israel, "locusts" refers to St. John's bread, the Carob tree.

Ravens feed Elijah: 1 Kings 17:2-6 "Then the word of the LORD came to him, saying, "Get away from here and turn eastward, and hide by the Brook Cherith, which flows into the Jordan. And it will be *that* you shall drink from the brook, and I have commanded the ravens to feed you there." So he went and did according to the word of the LORD, for he went and stayed by the Brook Cherith, which flows into the Jordan. The ravens brought him bread and meat in the morning, and bread and meat in the evening; and he drank from the brook."

To the average reader, this would seem like ravens, as in birds, are actually feeding Elijah. However, if that's the case, then there is a major contradiction that God would send a bird that He considered unclean to feed Elijah.

Leviticus 11:13-15 "'And these you shall regard as an abomination among the birds; they shall not be eaten, they *are* an abomination: the eagle, the vulture, the buzzard, the kite, and the falcon after its kind; every raven after its kind"

The Indigenous Bedouins of the land fed Elijah, and these Bedouins just happen to be called "ravens." The Bedouins live in tents in the desert that are covered with black cloth. What's interesting is that if you are overlooking a Bedouin encampment of black tents, they look like a flock of "ravens."

When a Rooster is Not a Chicken: Matthew 26:34 "Jesus said to him, "Assuredly, I say to you that this night, before the rooster crows, you will deny Me three times."

Matthew 26:69-75 "Now Peter sat outside in the courtyard. And a servant girl came to him, saying, "You also were with Jesus of Galilee." But he denied it before *them* all, saying, "I do not know what you are saying." And when he had gone out to the gateway, another *girl* saw him and said to those *who were* there, "This *fellow* also was with Jesus of Nazareth." But again he denied with an oath, "I do not know the Man!" And a little later those who stood by came up and said to Peter, "Surely you also are *one* of them, for your speech betrays you." Then he began to curse and swear, *saying,* "I do not know the Man!" Immediately a rooster crowed. And Peter remembered the word of Jesus who had said to him, "Before the rooster crows, you will deny Me three times." So he went out and wept bitterly."

I've watched several portrayals of this scene unfold in different movies concerning Peter denying Jesus. In every one of these portrayals, as soon as Peter denies Jesus the 3rd time, sure enough, we hear the rooster crowing! After all, the Bible does say that the cock crowed! But there's just one problem. Chickens were not allowed in the city of Jerusalem.

The Mishnah, which is the earliest compilation of rabbinic oral law, states that roosters (chickens) may not be raised in Jerusalem due to purity concerns (*m. Bava Kamma* 7.7; see also *b. Bava Kamma* 82b). This decree comes from the first century when the Temple stood in Jerusalem. So, if roosters were not permitted to be raised in Jerusalem, what or who was doing the crowing?

Eusebius, Bishop of Caesarea, is known as the "Father of Church History," and Papias, Bishop of Hierapolis, both point out that the book of Matthew was written in **Hebrew**! Therefore, this needs to be looked at from a **Hebraic** perspective. The word "גֶּבֶר" (gever) can mean man or rooster in Hebrew. The Greek word used here is "αλεκτορα" (alektor), which can also mean a man or rooster. However, the cock in this passage was not a rooster but a man called "the Temple Crier," and it was his job to announce that the Temple was open for service for the day by giving a three-fold trumpet blast.

Excavations around the Temple Mount in Jerusalem uncovered a stone bearing a **Hebrew** inscription "to the place of trumpeting." Scholars have suggested that this stone marked an area on the southwestern corner of the Temple Mount, facing toward the city, where priests would blow the trumpet or shofar, announcing the different times of the day and week (see Josephus, *War* 4.582). So what has been perceived as a "rooster" turns out to be a man called a "Temple Crier."

Nakedness of the Father: Have you ever wondered why Noah cursed Canaan? It's often taught that Ham sodomized Noah or just literally saw him naked. However, the Bible reveals what really happened!

Genesis 9:21-25 "Then he drank of the wine and was drunk, and became uncovered in his tent. And Ham, the father of Canaan, saw the nakedness of his father and told his two brothers outside. But Shem and Japheth took a garment, laid *it* on both their shoulders, and went backward and covered the nakedness of their father. Their faces *were* turned away, and they did not see their father's nakedness. So Noah awoke from his wine and knew what his younger son had done to him."

In Leviticus, we are told that having sexual relations with the wife of your father is considered "uncovering his nakedness."

Leviticus 18:8 "The nakedness of your father's wife you shall not uncover; it *is* your father's nakedness."

Leviticus 20:11 "The man who lies with his father's wife has uncovered his father's nakedness; both of them shall surely be put to death. Their blood *shall be* upon them."

Also, we know that the Book of Genesis was originally written in **Hebrew**. Therefore, it must be looked at from a Hebraic perspective to fully understand what is being read. The **Hebrew** language has male & female words. The word tent in **Hebrew** (אהל) is pronounced (**ohel**), which consists of Aleph (א), Hey (ה), and Lamed (ל). Remember, **Hebrew** is read from right to left. However, in this particular verse, the letter Hey (ה) is attached at the end of the word tent (**ohel**), thus making it feminine (אהלה).

Therefore, verse 21 suggests that Ham entered his mother's tent since the word tent is depicted as feminine. The verse tells us that Noah was drunk & naked. It's possible Noah passed out and/or was too drunk to do anything. Ham, noticing the situation, raped his mother & conceived Canaan. That is why Noah cursed Canaan!

Ham did not sodomize Noah; Ham had sex with his mother, and Canaan was the result!

Matthew 5:17: "Do not think that I came to destroy the Law or the Prophets. I did not come to destroy but to fulfill."

There has been some very harmful theology and doctrine come about over the last 1,900 years or so due to a misrepresentation of **Matthew 5:17**. Mainstream Christianity teaches that this verse means that the Torah, along with the other books of the "Old Testament," has become obsolete, or done away with. They say "all was fulfilled" when Jesus said, "it is finished," and the Law is no longer relevant. Such a belief about the Torah (law) could not be further from the truth.

Part of the problem is with our interpretation of "fulfil". In our Western cultural mindset, "fulfil" means to complete, finish, or put an end to. However, in a Hebraic cultural mindset, "fulfil" means to properly interpret. For example, take the word "replenish." In **Genesis 1:28**, God told Adam and Eve to replenish the earth. In our modern-day Western cultural mindset, we hear the word "replenish" and automatically think it means to fill up again. However, in the context of **Genesis 1:28**, "replenish" means to fill up completely!

Matthew 5:17 is actually a Hebrew idiom, which is a form of a figure of speech. "Destroy" and "fulfil" are technical terms used in rabbinic argumentation. When a sage felt that a colleague league had misinterpreted a passage of Scripture, he would say, "You are destroying the Law!" Needless to say, in most cases his colleague strongly disagreed. What was "destroying the Law" for one sage, was "fulfilling filling the Law" (correctly interpreting Scripture) for another.[14]

Just ask yourself one question. Do you consider the Ten Commandments relevant? The Ten Commandments are part of the Torah (law). Also, look at the first two words in verse 17; Jesus said **THINK NOT**! Interesting, Jesus says, don't even think it! So, really, Jesus said in **Matthew 5:17**, "THINK NOT," that I came to misinterpret the **teaching** or **instructions** of God, but I came to properly interpret. Also, look at verse **18**, "For assuredly, I say to you, till heaven and earth pass away, one jot or one tittle will by no means pass from the law till all is fulfilled." Heaven & earth are clearly still here!

2 Timothy 2:15 "Be diligent to present yourself approved to God, a worker who does not need to be ashamed, rightly dividing the word of truth."

As you can clearly see, there is quite a bit listed here that many people believe is actually in the Bible and has been misunderstood. While some of these things may seem harmless, if we give in to these subtle details, they can veer us off course and cause significant damage to our spiritual journey!

---

[14] David Bivin;Roy Blizzard Jr.. Understanding the Difficult Words of Jesus: New Insights From a Hebrew Perspective (Kindle Locations 912-914). Kindle Edition

HOW THE CHURCH LEFT ITS HEBRAIC ROOTS

Matthew 5:17 tells us, "Do not think that I came to destroy the Law or the Prophets. I did not come to destroy but to fulfill." Perry Stone stated, "Most Christians are not familiar with the Hebraic concept of the Bible, this despite the fact that most Christians understand that Jesus, the Apostles, the Prophets and the majority of other notables in the Bible were of Hebrew descent. This ignorance of the Hebraic nature of Scripture had led to much misunderstanding and, consequently and unfortunately, a degree of misinterpretation of the Scripture. This misunderstanding has affected how we think, and how we think affects our outlook on life, our doctrinal beliefs and our view of prophecy."[15]

"In the Hollywood movie Foxfire the celebrated actor Clint Eastwood is smuggled into Russia for the purpose of stealing Russia's most advanced fighter jet and flying it safely back to the U.S. Once Eastwood is smuggled into Russia he is taken to the home of two dissident Jewish engineers, a man and his wife, who have been involved in the development of the fastest plane in the world. Its highly technical 'brain' center was made with a thought-guided, thought-controlled weapons system that accepts human commands only in Russian. The pilot's thoughts are literally transmitted through his helmet to the computer.

Before Eastwood's character leaves for the Russian air base, he is briefed by the husband on how to operate the aircraft. After the briefing, he looks Eastwood straight in the eyes and says, "This is very important. When using your weapons you must think in Russian! You cannot think in English and

---

[15] Stone, Perry 40 Days of Teshuvah Page 1

transpose. You must think in Russian!" In much the same manner, when seeking to understand the most important Book ever written, you must think as a Jew. You cannot think in English and transpose. You must think as a Jew!"[16]

Being that we have a book written by Hebrews, about a Hebrew culture, in a Hebrew land, in a Hebrew language, from a Hebraic perspective, about a Hebrew Messiah, one would think that a Hebraic mentality would accompany all those in ministry as well as Christian believers. Dr. Brad Young says, "I think the church, I would say, for 2000 years the church has been teaching that the faith in Jesus cancels and replaces the faith of Jesus."[17] David Flusser writes, "Christianity arose among the Jews—it was once a part of Judaism. Therefore if you want to analyze Christian origins, you have to study ancient Judaism. As the Jewish roots of Christianity are patent, the obligation to include Jewish studies in the research of Christian origins is independent from the personal appreciation of both Judaism and Christianity by the scholar."[18]

The question then arises, how did the church get so far removed from its Hebraic roots? "Marcion (85-160 C.E.), the son of a bishop, who was also a wealthy shipbuilder, became a student of the Gnostic Christian Cerdo, who taught that there was a profound difference between the God of the Old Testament and the God of the New Testament. Like Cerdo, Marcion believed that Christianity was the only true religion. Like Cerdo, Marcion rejected everything Jewish in Scripture. And like Cerdo, Marcion believed that the God of the Old Testament was a harsh and lesser God than the "good God" revealed in the New Testament."[19]

In 139 C.E., "Marcion went to Rome and presented his anti-Jewish gospel to the congregation. He gave the congregation 200,000 sesterces. After reading Marcion's revision of the Apostolic Writings, the congregation gave back the money and excommunicated him from their fellowship, ruling Marcion to be a Heretic. Shortly after 139 C.E., due to the listing of "acceptable" writings according to Marcion, the Church was forced to begin the selection of which writings, circulating among

---

[16] Rhoades, Richard N. Faith of the Ages: The Hebraic Roots of the Christian Faith (p. 1). iUniverse. Kindle Edition.
[17] Did Jesus Speak Hebrew? | Dr. Brad Young
https://www.youtube.com/watch?v=5F_TRXvvH_Y
[18] Flusser, David. Judaism and the Origins of Christianity . Varda Books. Kindle Edition.
[19] Michael Silver, The Torah Is Valid, (Organ, NM: Tree of Life Publications, 2004), p. 187

congregations, would be authorized as Holy Scripture."[20] In essence, this way of thinking by Marcion created a snowball effect within Church history that caused major devastation to not just Jews and Gentiles but to the Church as a whole.

"Although the early Church identified Marcion as a heretic, today many theologians have accepted his views as sound doctrine. It was Marcion, however, who adopted **Matthew 5:17** as proof text that God's Law had been superseded by grace."[21] Historian E.C. Blackman has noted how Marcion changed the meaning of **Matthew 5:17** by "inverting the order of the clauses so as to give exactly an opposite sense."[22] According to Marcion's interpretation, Jesus said, "Think not that I have come to fulfill the Law, I have not come to fulfill but to abolish it."

Marcion was so convinced that Paul's message of grace was in opposition to the Torah ['Law'] that he created his own canon of the Bible and completely did away with the Old Testament, only keeping edited portions of Luke and edited portions of Paul's writings that agreed with his own theology. For Marcion, Paul was the only true Apostle. Marcion held that all the other Apostles had corrupted the teachings of Jesus by mixing them with Jewish customs.

Marcion rejected the books written by Matthew, Mark, and John because of Jewish influences. While he accepted the Book of Acts, he removed everything Jewish. Marcion also excluded 1st and 2nd Timothy, Titus, and Hebrews because of their Jewishness.[23] It is said that Marcion's misrepresentation of the Scriptures was so contrary to their true meaning that Polycarp, who was a student of John, called him the "firstborn of Satan."[24]

In 160 C.E., Justin Martyr wrote to the Jewish apologist Trypho, saying, "circumcision was given to you as a sign, that you may be separated from

---

[20] Rhoades, Richard N.. Faith of the Ages: The Hebraic Roots of the Christian Faith (p. 148). iUniverse. Kindle Edition.

[21] Mosley, Dr. Ron. Yeshua: A Guide to the Real Jesus and the Original Church (p. 87). Messianic Jewish Communications. Kindle Edition.

[22] E.C. Blackman, Marcion and His Influence (London: 1948), p. 50.

[23] Philip Schaff, History Of The Christian Church, (Grand Rapids, MI: William B. Eerdmans Publishing Company, 1910), Vol. 1, pp. 210-211.

[24] Elgin Moyer, The Wycliffe Biographical Dictionary Of The Church, (Chicago, IL: Moody Press, 1982), p. 263

other nations, and from us [Christians], and that you alone may suffer that which you now justly suffer, and that your land may be desolate, and your cities burnt with fire. These things have happened to you in fairness and justice."[25]

In 170 C.E., Irenaeus, who was said to be a disciple of Polycarp, held that the seventh day Sabbath was merely a symbol and belonged to the Jews.[26] Irenaeus later wrote: "the Jews, had they been cognizant of our [Christian] future existence, and that we should use these proofs from the Scriptures which declare that all other nations will inherit eternal life, but they who boast themselves as being the house of Jacob are disinherited from the grace of God, would never have hesitated themselves to burn their own Scriptures."[27]

Around 240 C.E., Tertullian taught that it was the Jews who stirred up the pagan persecution of Christians, saying, "the synagogues were the seed-plot of all the calumny against Christians"[28] Around 245 C.E. Origin viewed the seventh day Sabbath, the appointed festivals, and Jewish customs as legalistic and belonging to the Jews only. For Origin, Christianity was the pure religion of God.[29]

In 300 C.E., Eusebius, bishop of Caesarea, is known as the "Father of Church History," who was a loyal supporter of the sun-worshiper Constantine, who had no love for the Jews. In citing the historical relationship between the patriarchs Abraham, Isaac, and Jacob and Christians, Eusebius made a sharp distinction between Hebrews and Jews. He maintained that though they themselves were not Jews, neither were they Gentiles. Rather, says Eusebius, "from the beginning they were Christians, and led a Christian life."[30]

In 325 C.E., The Council of Nicea convened, presided by the anti-Jewish Emperor Constantine, decreed under the penalty of death to anyone who

---

[25] Dialogue with Trypho, Chapter XVI.
[26] Philip Schaff, History Of The Christian Church, (Grand Rapids, MI: William B. Eerdmans Publishing Company, 1910), Vol. 2, p. 204
[27] Irenaeus, Contra Haereses, III, XXI; P.G., VII, p. 946.
[28] Tertullian, de Spectaculis, XXX; P.L., I, p. 662.
[29] Paul J. Glenn, The History Of Philosophy, (St. Louis, MO: B. Herder Book Co., 1929), p. 154.
[30] James Parkes, The Conflict of the Church and the Synagogue: A Study in the Origins of Antisemitism, (New York, NY: Atheneum, 1977), pp. 161-162.

adds or changes the creed of Nicea, which included the abolishment of Passover for "the more legitimate festival of Easter." Constantine put the nail in the coffin concerning the Jewishness of our roots. Constantine basically outlawed everything Jewish.

In 345 C.E., John Chrysostom, the gifted bishop, and orator of the Church in Antioch, who was no lover of the Jews or their Judaic faith, said: "I hate the Jews. For they have the Law and they insult it."[31] Chrysostom later added: "the fact that the Holy Books of the Law are to be found in the synagogues makes them more detestable, for the Jews have simply introduced these Books, not to honour them, but to insult them, and dishonor them"; "the Jews do not worship God but devils, so that all their feasts are unclean"; "God hates them [Jews], and indeed has always hated them. But since the murder of Jesus He allows them no time for repentance"; "It was of set purpose that He concentrated all their worship in Jerusalem that He might more easily destroy it"; "It was not by their [Jews] power that the Caesars did what they did to you: it was done by the wrath of God, and His absolute rejection of you"; "It is childish in the face of this absolute rejection to imagine that God will ever allow the Jews to rebuild their Temple or to return to Jerusalem"; "When it is clear that God hates them, it is the duty of Christians to hate them too"[32]

Regarding Chrysostom, Michael Brown said, "But there's something just as shocking as Chrysostom's words, which can be multiplied. It's the fact that most Christians have no idea he ever said them, including pastors who have studied in seminary. In fact, on more than one occasion while teaching at a leading seminary I asked one of the Church historians, "So, when do you teach on Chrysostom's sermons against the Jews?" The answer was always the same (spoken with some shame as well): "We don't.""[33]

Between 354-430 C.E., The Catholic Monk Augustine took Marcion's theology of grace opposing God's Law and applied it to his own theology. Augustine also believed that the Law was done away with the coming of Christ and maintained that the Christian Sabbath, Sunday, was derived from

---

[31] James Parkes, The Conflict of the Church and the Synagogue: A Study in the Origins of Antisemitism, (New York, NY: Atheneum, 1977), pp. 165-166.
[32] Chrysostom, Against Judaizing Christians, Ser. I, III, IV, V, VI.
[33] Brown, Michael L.. Our Hands are Stained with Blood (pp. 27-28). Destiny Image, Inc.. Kindle Edition.

the resurrection of Christ, not from the Fourth Commandment. Philip Schaff says: "Augustine struggled from the Manichaean heresy into catholic orthodoxy.... Augustine put the church above the Word, and established the principle of catholic tradition."[34] Augustine also believed that the Septuagint trumped the original Hebrew because it was an updated translation; therefore, he believed it to be inspired. In that way of thinking, Augustine made the original Hebrew text errant instead of inerrant. In the early days of his Christian faith, Augustine (354-430) was premillennial. However, through time, he abandoned the idea of a literal return of Christ to establish a physical kingdom on earth. He used this new allegorical method of interpretation to explain away the literal return of Christ, and thus, amillennialism was born. In his book, *The City of God*, Augustine taught that the Universal Church is the Messianic Kingdom and that the millennium began with Christ's first coming. When the church lost the hope of the imminent return of Christ, it plunged headlong into the dark ages. The seeds of false interpretation bore fruit, giving rise to Roman Catholicism and a works-based religion. Augustine's amillennial teaching continued to be the standard view of organized Christendom until the 17th century.

In 382 C.E., Jerome was commissioned by Pope Damasus I to revise old Latin translations. Jerome's Latin Vulgate Bible became the definitive and officially promulgated Latin version of the Bible of the Roman Catholic Church. Repudiating the Jewishness of the Scriptures, Jerome wrote: "For the grace of the Law which hath passed away we have received the abiding grace of the Gospel; for the shadows and figures of the Old Testament we have the Truth of Jesus Christ."[35]

In the early 1500s, when Martin Luther broke away from the Catholic Church, he acknowledged that Jesus was a Jew. Luther wrote, "Perhaps I will attract some of the Jews to the Christian faith. For our fools—the popes, bishops, sophists, and monks the coarse blockheads!—have until this time so treated the Jews that...if I had been a Jew and had seen such idiots and blockheads ruling and teaching the Christian religion, I would rather have been a sow than a Christian. For they have dealt with the Jews as if they were dogs and not human beings."[36]

---

[34] Philip Schaff, History Of The Christian Church, (Grand Rapids, MI: William B. Eerdmans Publishing Company, 1910), Vol. 7, pp. 737-738
[35] Jerome, Adv. Pelog. I. 31, P.L. XXIII
[36] Martin Luther, That Jesus Christ Was Born a Jew, reprinted in Frank Ephraim Talmage, ed., Disputation and Dialogue: Readings in the Jewish-Christian Encounter (New York: Ktav/Anti-Defamation League of B'nai B'rith, 1975), 33.

Around 20 years later, Luther changed his attitude towards the Jews when they did not convert and see his way of thinking. Luther wrote, "First, their synagogues should be set on fire.... Secondly, their homes should likewise be broken down and destroyed.... Thirdly, they should be deprived of their prayer-books and Talmud's.... Fourthly, their rabbis must be forbidden under threat of death to teach any more.... Fifthly, passport and traveling privileges should be absolutely for bidden to the Jews....Sixthly, they ought to be stopped from usury [charging interest on loans].... Seventhly, let the young and strong Jews and Jewesses be given the flail, the ax, the hoe, the spade, the distaff, and spindle, and let them earn their bread by the sweat of their noses.... We ought to drive the rascally lazy bones out of our system.... Therefore away with them.... To sum up, dear princes and nobles who have Jews in your domains, if this advice of mine does not suit you, then find a better one so that you and we may all be free of this insufferable devilish burden—the Jews."[37]

In 1933, the German Lutheran Gerhard Kittel, one of the great New Testament scholars of the day, published a book outlining how his country must handle the "Jewish question." Extermination would be impractical. (Later he added that it would also be unchristian.) Zionism was out of the question. (There were too many Jews to fit in Palestine, and the Arabs would not be happy with the situation anyway.) Assimilation would be the worst solution of all. That would corrupt the German race! Rather, the Jews should accept discrimination and defamation as their lot. Let them be treated as "guests" in a foreign land—second class, beleaguered guests, of course. After all, they were Jews, weren't they? In fact, according to Kittel, the only authentic Jews were those "who in obedience...take on themselves the suffering of dispersal...authentic Judaism abides by the symbol of the stranger wandering restless and homeless on the face of the earth."[38]

Regarding Kittel, Robert P. Ericksen wrote,...resurrected Christian antisemitism from the Middle Ages, refurbished it with a touch of contemporary racial mysticism, and raised it as a German, Christian bulwark against the Jewish menace.... [He] proposed harsh measures to

---

[37] Martin Luther, Concerning the Jews and Their Lies, reprinted in Talmage, Disputation and Dialogue, p 34-36.
[38] Gerhard Kittel, from his book Die Judenfrage ("The Jewish Question"), quoted in Charlotte Klein, Anti-Judaism in Christian Theology (trans. by Edward Quinn, Philadelphia: Fortress Press, 1978), 12-13.

deal with [this menace], and he directed his research to reveal Jewish degeneracy. In short, he swam in the Nazi stream, though he may have preferred a different stroke.[39]

Luther had asked the question, "What shall we Christians do now with this rejected, cursed people, the Jews?" Fast forward around 400 years, Adolph Hitler, in Mein Kampf, gave the answer: "…it is the inexorable Jew who struggles for his domination over the nations. No nation can remove this hand from its throat except by the sword."[40] Hitler and his regime killed two-thirds of Europe's Jews!

Today, many of our modern Theologians, such as Andy Stanley, have stated that we need to unhitch from the Old Testament. In response, Pastor Scott Stewart said, "If we are supposed to unhook ourselves from the Jewish Scriptures, then the Apostles didn't know that because they bring the Jewish Scriptures into the New Testament." [41]

Many believers of Jesus believe that Jesus is only shown in the New Testament. Due to this way of thinking, believers severely disable themselves by only seeing what is taught in large by a Western-centered mentality. When the Church proclaims a Gospel without its Jewishness restored, she is at best failing to proclaim "the whole counsel of God" (Acts 20:27). At worst, she may be communicating what Paul called "another Gospel" (Galatians 1:6-9).[42]

Dr. Bill Barrick said, "The New Testament is God's commentary on the Old Testament, therefore if we rightly interpreted the Old Testament it should not be in contradiction to God's commentary in the New Testament."[43] I previously used this analogy in a previous writing, "If you

---

[39] Robert P. Ericksen, Theologians Under Hitler (New Haven: Yale Univ. Press, 1985), 76,74.
[40] Cited in Christopher J. Probst, Demonizing the Jews: Luther and the Protestant Church in Germany (Bloomington and Indianapolis: Indiana University Press, 2012)
[41] September 4, 2022 • Scott Stewart
https://aclr.org/archive?sapurl=LysxM2I1L2xiL21pLytzbjh4ZHozP2JyYW5kaW5nPXRydW UmZW1iZWQ9dHJ1ZSZyZWNlbnRSb3V0ZT1hcHAud2ViLWFwcC5saWJyYXJ5Lmxppc3Qmc mVjZW50Um91dGVTbHVnPSUyQnR0N2tocWWg=
[42] Restoring The Jewishness of the Gospel: A Message for Christians Condensed from Messianic Judaism . Messianic Jewish Communications. Kindle Edition.
[43] Lecture 1: Old Testament Introduction - Dr. Bill Barrick
https://www.youtube.com/watch?v=VT7C9QUnMJY&t=5578s

are traveling true north but along the way your path ends up shifting by one degree, you are still traveling north, but not true north. Now imagine traveling along that same path for 2,000 years. You would be quite a ways off from true north. This is why it is so important for each & every one of us to rightly divide the word of truth."[44] It's important to know what the Bible teaches, not what people think it teaches.

It's important to remember that everything has an origin or a root. It's important to trace things back to their original root because where ignorance exists, myths flourish! Once you go to the root, you find the fruit. If you remove the Root, you remove the fruit! **Colossians 2:6-7** says, "As you therefore have received Christ Jesus the Lord, so walk in Him, rooted and built up in Him and established in the faith, as you have been taught, abounding in it with thanksgiving."

---

[44] Rice, Jay. Wait, That's Not In The Bible? (p. 10). Kindle Edition.

CROSSING OVER

Romans 11:13-20 "For I speak to you Gentiles, inasmuch as I am an apostle **(The Hebrew word for "apostle" is שָׁלִיחַ (shaliach) which means one sent with a message)** to the Gentiles, I magnify my ministry, If by any means I may provoke to jealousy *them which are* **my flesh (Jews)**, and might save some of them. For if their being cast away is the reconciling of the world, what *will* **their (Jews)** *acceptance be but life from the dead?* For if the firstfruit *be* holy, the lump *is* also *holy:* and if the **root (Hebrew)***be* holy, so *are* the branches. And if some of the branches were broken off, and you, being a wild olive tree, were grafted in among **them (Jews)**, and with **them (Jews)** became a partaker of the **root (Hebrew)** and **fatness (Richness, Goodness, or the Fruit)** of the olive tree, do not boast against the branches. But if you do boast, *remember that* you do not support the **root**, but the **root** supports you. You will say then, "Branches were broken off that I might be grafted in." Well *said.* Because of unbelief they were broken off, and you stand by faith. Do not be haughty, but fear."

Our faith in its most technical sense is the Judeo-Christian faith. Have you ever asked yourself, "What do I know about the Judeo side of my faith?" Christianity is rooted in Judaism, and once it is reconnected to its roots, the picture becomes much clearer of what God was trying to convey to His church. Unfortunately, mainstream Christianity has more or less detached itself from its Judeo root, the Tanakh, which is the Hebrew word for (Old Testament), otherwise known as the "Hebrew Scriptures," and is the foundation for both Judaism and Christianity. It's been said that Judaism doesn't need Christianity to explain itself, but Christianity cannot explain itself without Judaism. However, both Judaism and Christianity are nothing without Jesus since Jesus is the Word!

Have you ever bought a movie or a novel that you had never seen or read and intentionally began watching the movie or reading the novel right in the middle? Sounds weird, right? Unfortunately, that has become somewhat of the norm within mainstream Christianity regarding the Bible.

This is yet another example of the illusory truth effect. Mainstream Christianity teaches people to mainly study and focus primarily on the New Testament, otherwise known as the "Apostolic Scriptures" (Brit Chadashah), which in Hebrew means **"Covenant Renewed."** The problem is that much is missed without connecting it to its foundation, the Tanakh (Old Testament), and much has been taken out of context. **And remember what I stated earlier when you remove the text from "context," you're left with a "con"!**

Imagine you have a house. The New Testament represents the roof and four walls; the Old Testament is the Foundation! So, if you have the foundation, which is the Tanakh (Old Testament), then the Covenant Renewed makes much more sense.

Many churches call themselves the so-called "New Testament church". Pastors and churches who have this "New Testament church" mindset, for the most part, believe and teach that the Tanakh (Old Testament) is done away with and obsolete, which is a form of replacement theology. This mindset implores people to begin reading the Bible from the middle, beginning with the Brit Chadashah (New Testament), "Covenant Renewed," instead of the beginning of the Bible itself with the Tanakh (Old Testament), the "Hebrew Scriptures."

This "New Testament church" mindset, along with many others believes that the story of Jesus begins in the Brit Chadashah (New Testament), which is the middle of the book. However, the story of Jesus begins in the Tanakh (Old Testament). **John 5:46-47** Jesus said, "For if you believed Moses, you would believe me: for **he wrote of me**. But if you do not believe his writings, how will you believe my words?" **Did you see that? Jesus said that Moses wrote of him.**

We know that Moses wrote the first five books of the Bible, which is called Torah in Hebrew and Pentateuch in Greek. Also, take a look at the road to Emmaus. **Luke 24:27** "And beginning at Moses and all the prophets, **he expounded to them in all the scriptures the things concerning himself.**" And then Luke **24:44-45**, "Then He said to them, "These *are* the words which I spoke to you while I was still with you, that all things must be fulfilled which were written in the Law of Moses and *the* Prophets and *the* Psalms concerning Me." **And He opened their understanding, that they might comprehend the Scriptures."**

If Jesus helped the disciples to understand the Scriptures, then that means He wants all of us to understand it! Because it all points to Him! You see, even Jesus is telling us that The Old Testament is the story of Himself! So if Jesus can find himself in Moses, the prophets, the psalms, and all the scriptures, then we should want to find him there as well! After all, Jesus told us to learn of himself. **Matthew 11:29** "Take my yoke upon you, and **learn from me;"**

And look at **John 1:1-3** and **John 1:14**. **John 1:1-3 "In the beginning was the Word, and the Word was with God, and the Word was God**. He was in the beginning with God. All things were made through Him, and without Him nothing was made that was made." **John 1:14 "And the Word was made flesh, and dwelt among us,** (and we beheld his glory, the glory as of the only begotten of the Father,) full of grace and truth."

John is literally telling you where to go, which is back to the beginning! It is important to realize that the only thing that separates the Old Testament from the New Testament is 400 years and a piece of paper. **It's all one book!**

Unfortunately, many Christian pastors, colleges, seminaries, and church congregations have severed themselves from that Hebraic root, which is why we have nearly 50k Christian denominations. No wonder people are confused. The same people the church is so desperate to reach has to wonder why there is a church on every corner and we can't seem to get it together. Instead of changing the culture, it seems the church has been changed by the culture. Instead of declaring a better way of life the church shouts to the world, "Join us and we will teach you our way of life which includes all of our own rules and regulations and interpretations of Scripture."[45]

When the root is severed, it prohibits from partaking in the fatness, which is the fruit, richness, and goodness! Since the Hebraic root has been severed, a Greek way of thinking has become the mainstream. Greek has its place. However, the problem is that many Christian pastors, colleges, seminaries, and church congregations hold Greek as the foundation for studying the Bible, which is unfortunate because, without Hebrew as the foundation, along with Hebraic training, much is missed. Also, if we only view and study the Bible through a Greek lens, western mindset, or filter, then we become severely disabled in trying to understand what God is trying to convey through His Hebraic mindset.

This is basically a form of replacement theology, and with replacement theology comes a replacement of who Jesus and Paul are, which creates a spiritual schizophrenic mindset, which is one reason why Jews aren't interested in Jesus! Much of the church over the course of the last 1,900 years or so has stripped the identity of who Jesus really is, a Hebrew! This

---

[45] Miller, Dwain. Jesus the Rabbi: Unlocking the Hebraic Teaching of Yeshua (p. 53). Kindle Edition.

spiritual schizophrenic mindset, for the most part, has caused many followers of Jesus to not really understand who they are and who they have become, which is **Hebrew!**

Am I saying that in order to know God that, you have be a scholar in Hebrew? Not at all! God's love is so vast and infinite that He has and continues to allow Himself to be known by all ethnicities, races, creeds, and languages. **But why would anyone truly in love with Jesus just be satisfied with a surface understanding of the Bible?** The point that I'm trying to make is that once we realize our true identity in Jesus, our relationship with Him becomes so much more intimate!

When someone decides to walk in the Hebraic perspective of their Christian faith, that does not mean they are rejecting Jesus. Nor does it mean that they want to become Jewish. It simply means that they are attempting to do Bible things in Bible ways and walk as close to Him as possible. After all, Jesus said "Follow Me" at least 13 times in the Gospels. **Jeremiah 6:16** "Thus saith the LORD, Stand ye in the ways, and see, and ask for the old paths, where *is* the good way, and walk therein, and ye shall find rest for your souls..." ``The Gospels are rife with misunderstanding," explain Bivin and Blizzard. ``...had the Church been provided with a proper Hebraic understanding of the words of Jesus, most theological controversies would never have arisen in the first place."[46]

Identification Leads to Revelation

Seven times in the Bible, God tells us not to be ignorant. Two out of these seven ignorant statements deal with identification. The first statement we will look at is **1Corinthians 10:1-4** "Moreover, brethren, I would not that ye should be **ignorant**, how that all our fathers were under the cloud, and all passed through the sea; And were all baptized unto Moses in the cloud and in the sea; And did all eat the same spiritual meat; and did all drink the same spiritual drink: for they drank of that spiritual Rock that followed them: and that Rock was Christ."

Here, we see Paul speaking to the Corinthians in Corinth. He tells them that he does not want them to be ignorant of the fact that their fathers, their ancestors, were with Moses at the parting of the Red Sea. But how could that be since Corinth did not exist at the time of the parting of the Red Sea?

It's because they became believers in Jesus and were grafted into the

---

[46] David Bivin;Roy Blizzard Jr.. Understanding the Difficult Words of Jesus: New Insights From a Hebrew Perspective (Kindle Location 511). Kindle Edition.

same Olive tree as their fellow Jews, partaking of the same **root**! And that root is **Hebrew**! Paul is letting the Corinthians know that Hebrew history becomes their history since they have accepted Jesus as their Lord and Savior! The same concept applies to us as well. When we become followers of Jesus, Hebrew history becomes our history. We identify that history as a part of our family and heritage. This will become even clearer as we dive a little deeper.

The second ignorant statement dealing with identification occurs just two chapters later. **1 Corinthians 12:1-2** "Now concerning spiritual *gifts,* brethren**, I would not have you ignorant. Ye know that ye were Gentiles**, carried away unto these dumb idols, even as ye were led."

Paul here makes the statement that you "were" Gentiles. Meaning you were Gentiles, but you are not Gentiles anymore! The word Gentiles is Goyim (גויים) in Hebrew, which means nations; however, it also means Pagans. Often, we may hear someone make the statement, "We are gentile believers." This is why it's important to look at these words from a biblical perspective because you have these people saying, "We are pagan believers." Sounds weird, right? Since we are no longer Gentiles, we are a part of something much bigger!

Moving on, take a look at **Ephesians 2:11-20** "**Wherefore remember, that ye being in time past Gentiles** in the flesh, who are called Uncircumcision by that which is called the Circumcision in the flesh made by hands; **That at that time ye were without Christ, being aliens from the commonwealth of Israel, and strangers from the covenants of promise, having no hope, and without God in the world: But now in Christ Jesus ye who sometimes were far off are made nigh by the blood of Christ.** For he is our peace, who hath made **both one**, and hath broken down the middle wall of partition between us; Having abolished in his flesh the enmity, even the law of commandments contained in ordinances; for to make in himself of twain one new man, so making peace; And that he might reconcile both unto God in **one body** by the cross, having slain the enmity thereby: And came and preached peace to you which were afar off, and to them that were nigh. For through him we both have access by one Spirit unto the Father. Now **therefore ye are no more strangers and foreigners**, but fellow citizens with the saints, and of the household of God; **And are built upon the foundation of the apostles and prophets, Jesus Christ himself being the chief corner** *stone;*"

Ephesians 2:11-20 says that **you were Gentiles** and aliens from the commonwealth of Israel & **you were strangers from the Covenants** of promise, **but not anymore!**

Then take a look at **1 Peter 2:10** "Which in time past *were* not a people,

but *are* now the people of God: which had not obtained mercy, but now have obtained mercy."

Galatians 3:28-29 "There is neither Jew nor Greek, there is neither slave nor free, there is neither male nor female—**for you are all one in Messiah Yeshua.** And if you belong to Messiah, then **you are Abraham's seed—heirs according to the promise."**

Paul states that "the Gentiles are heirs together with Israel, members together of one body" **(Eph. 3:6b)**. Hence, Gentiles have a new history—Israel's history is now their history. In writing to the predominantly gentile church of Corinth, Paul states that the ancient Israelites were the forebears of the Corinthians: "our forefathers were all under the cloud, and ... they all passed through the sea" **(1 Cor. 10:1)**. In the early Church, therefore, Jew and Gentile claimed a common spiritual ancestry with the Hebrews of old.[47]

The Bible was written by Hebrew people in the Hebrew language, set in a Hebrew culture, positioned in a Hebrew nation, and was about a Hebrew Messiah. Our root system could not be more transparent. As Pastor Scott Stewart says, "When you go to the root (origin), you find the fruit!" It's important to look at the Bible from God's perspective, not mans!

Up to this point, we have mentioned Hebrew and Hebraic perspectives quite a bit. So what is Hebrew, and why does it matter? Not only is Hebrew one of the world's languages, but Hebrew is more than likely the oldest language in the world. However, it's not just any language; it's the language of God Himself. But Hebrew is much more than a language. Hebrew is, in essence, God's character, nature, culture, and identity. The more we understand Hebrew as an identity, the better we can understand and relate to the language and culture of Hebrew. Which will, in turn, help us to better understand the Bible and understand that Jesus Himself is Hebrew.

So, what does "Hebrew" mean? The following three words are connected as the root (Ayin-Bet-Resh עבר) Hebrew, read from right to left.

H5674 – עבר – ʻâbar Brown-Driver-Briggs Dictionary Definition: *to pass over or by or through, alienate, bring, carry, do away, take, take away, transgress*
to pass over, cross, cross over, pass over, march over, overflow, go over, to pass beyond, to pass through, traverse, passers-through, to pass through, to pass along, pass by, overtake and pass, sweep by, passer-by, to be past,

---

[47] Wilson, Marvin R.. Our Father Abraham: Jewish Roots of the Christian Faith (p. 9). Wm. B. Eerdmans Publishing Co.. Kindle Edition.

be over, to pass on, go on, pass on before, go in advance of, pass along, travel, advance, to pass away, to emigrate, leave (one's territory), to vanish, to perish, cease to exist, to become invalid, become obsolete (of law, decree), to be alienated, pass into other hands, to be crossed, to impregnate, cause to cross, to cause to pass over, cause to bring over, cause to cross over, make over to, dedicate, devote, to cause to pass through, to cause to pass by or beyond or under, let pass by, to cause to pass away, cause to take away, to pass over

H5676 – עבר – ʻêber Brown-Driver-Briggs Dictionary Definition: *region beyond or across, side, opposite side*

H5680 – עברי – ʻibrîy - **Ibri** Brown-Driver-Briggs Dictionary Definition: *"one from beyond"*

Hebrew simply means to "cross over," "pass over," or "one from beyond." The first time we see the term "Hebrew" in English is in **Genesis 14:13,** where Abram was the first person to be called a "**Hebrew**." **Genesis 14:13** "And there came one that had escaped, and told Abram the **Hebrew**;"

However, the first time "**Hebrew**" is used in the Bible is in **Genesis 12:6** "And Abram **passed through** (H5674 – עבר – ʻâbar) the land unto the place of Sichem, unto the plain of Moreh. And the Canaanite was then in the land." Abraham was the original Hebrew. Abraham did not have Jewish parents; he was a gentile, yet he became a Hebrew, the father of the Jewish people.

God's chosen people also identified themselves as "**Hebrews**" both in the Tanakh (Old Testament) **Jonah 1:9** "And he said unto them, I *am* an **Hebrew**; and I fear the LORD, the God of heaven, which hath made the sea and the dry *land.*" As well as in the Brit Chadashah (Covenant Renewed), **Philippians 3:5** "Circumcised the eighth day, of the stock of Israel, *of* the tribe of Benjamin, an **Hebrew** of the **Hebrews**; as touching the law, a Pharisee;"

Joshua 24:2-3 "And Joshua said unto all the people, Thus saith the LORD God of Israel, Your fathers dwelt on **the other side** of the flood in old time, even Terah, the father of Abraham, and the father of Nachor: and they served other gods. And I took your father Abraham from **the other side** of the flood, and led him throughout all the land of Canaan, and multiplied his seed, and gave him Isaac."

Joshua 24:8 "And I brought you into the land of the Amorites, which dwelt **on the other side** Jordan; and they fought with you: and I gave them into your hand, that ye might possess their land; and I destroyed them from before you."

Joshua 24:14-15 "Now therefore fear the LORD, and serve him in sincerity and in truth: and put away the gods which your fathers served **on the other side of the flood**, and in Egypt; and serve ye the LORD. And if it seem evil unto you to serve the LORD, choose you this day whom ye will serve; whether the gods which your fathers served that were **on the other side of the flood**, or the gods of the Amorites, in whose land ye dwell: but as for me and my house, we will serve the LORD."

In the above passages, Joshua distinguishes between Abram before he passes over and the life he is called to live after he **"crossed over."** Abram was a Gentile who served other gods beyond the river, but when he **"crossed over,"** he was committed to God. Here, when Joshua is speaking of **the other side**, he is using (H5676 – עבר – ʻêber – Eber)

This transformative journey is repeated with Israel as they cross the Red Sea towards freedom and again as they cross the Jordan River towards the promised land. "Passing over" was a distinct feature of God's people. "Passing over" or "Crossing over" the waters, as much as it is a physical act, also signifies a symbolic act of leaving the past behind and starting a renewed life. This profound transformation is enacted in the Baptism that each of us goes through as young believers as well.

When God speaks to Moses about the **Passover** sacrifice, He says that He will **Pass Over** the land using the same word (H5674 – עבר – ʻâbar), which is connected to "Ivri" Hebrew, as seen below.

Exodus 12:12 "For I will **pass through** the land of Egypt this night, and will smite all the firstborn in the land of Egypt, both man and beast; and against all the gods of Egypt I will execute judgment: I am the LORD."

Exodus 12:23 "For the LORD will **pass through** to smite the Egyptians; and when he seeth the blood upon the lintel, and on the two side posts, the LORD will pass over the door, and will not suffer the destroyer to come in unto your houses to smite you."

We see the same word (H5674 – עבר – ʻâbar), which is connected to "Ivri" Hebrew, used again in the Song of Moses after the Hebrews cross the Red Sea.

Exodus 15:16 "Fear and dread shall fall upon them; by the greatness of thine arm they shall be as still as a stone; till thy people **pass over**, O LORD, till the people **pass over**, which thou hast purchased."

Jesus tells us that whoever hears Him and puts their trust in God will pass from death to life. When you accept Jesus as your Lord and Savior, you "**Cross Over**" or (**Iber**), you become **Hebrew**. The Bible tells us that we as believers have been translated, or "crossed over," from darkness to light.

John 5:24 "Most assuredly, I say to you, he who hears My word and believes in Him who sent Me has everlasting life, and shall not come into judgment, but has **passed** from death into life. "

1 John 3:14 " We know that we have **passed** from death to life, because we love the brethren. He who does not love *his* brother abides in death."

Colossians 1:13 "Who hath delivered us from the power of darkness, and hath **translated** *us* into the kingdom of his dear Son:"

1 Peter 2:9-10 "But ye *are* a chosen generation, a royal priesthood, an holy nation, a peculiar people; that ye should shew forth the praises of him who hath **called you out of darkness into his marvellous light: Which in time past** *were* **not a people, but** *are* **now the people of God**: which had not obtained mercy, but now have obtained mercy."

Ephesians 5:8 "**For you were once darkness, but now** *you are* **light in the Lord.** Walk as children of light "

Acts 26:14-18 " And when we all had fallen to the ground, I heard a voice speaking to me and saying in the **Hebrew language**, 'Saul, Saul, why are you persecuting Me? *It is* hard for you to kick against the goads.' (**Paul goes out of his way to say Jesus is speaking Hebrew**) So I said, 'Who are You, Lord?' And He said, 'I am Jesus, whom you are persecuting. But rise and stand on your feet; for I have appeared to you for this purpose, to make you a minister and a witness both of the things which you have seen and of the things which I will yet reveal to you. I will deliver you from the *Jewish* people, as well as *from* the Gentiles, to whom I now send you, to open their eyes, *in order* **to turn** *them* **from darkness to light, and** *from* **the power of Satan to God**, that they may receive forgiveness of sins and an inheritance among those who are sanctified by faith in Me."

In essence, the **Hebrew** is a person who has "**crossed over**" from darkness to light, from death to life, from a life of sin to a life of righteousness through God's Commands, from obeying false gods to obeying the one true Creator of the universe. So now it becomes clear why Abram was called a **Hebrew**. This characteristic of "**crossing over**" or "**passing over**" becomes part of the **Hebrew** experience and is seen as part of the process regarding the journey of God's people.

The Bible is God's message to us. We know that paying attention to God's words is important; however, when the Bible says something repeatedly, it's God's way of really trying to get your attention. Sometimes, He repeats the same message with the same words, such as "His love endures forever" in every verse of **Psalm 136**. Sometimes, the same thought recurs with almost endless variation, such as the psalmist's love for the law of God in **Psalm 119**. There are also several verses in the Bible that speak about believers in Jesus having the same mindset, being likeminded, **or thinking alike.**

Romans 15:5-6 "Now the God of patience and consolation grant you to be **likeminded one toward another according to Christ Jesus**: That ye may with **one mind** *and* **one mouth** glorify God, even the Father of our Lord Jesus Christ."

1 Corinthians 1:10 "Now I beseech you, brethren, by the name of our Lord Jesus Christ, that **ye all speak the same thing, and** *that* **there be no divisions among you; but** *that* **ye be perfectly joined together in the same mind and in the same judgment."**

1 Corinthians 2:16 "For who hath known the mind of the Lord, that he may instruct him? **But we have the mind of Christ."**

Philippians 2:2 "Fulfil ye my joy, **that ye be likeminded, having the same love,** *being* **of one accord, of one mind**."

In **John 10:30**, Jesus said, "I and my Father are one." In John chapter 17, Jesus is about to be arrested. Jesus is praying to the Father, and five times, He prays that we would all be one, as He and the Father are one.

John 17:11 "And now I am no more in the world, but these are in the world, and I come to thee. Holy Father, keep through thine own name those whom thou hast given me, that they may be **one,** as we *are*."

John 17:20-23 "Neither pray I for these alone, but for them also which shall believe on me through their word; That they all may be **one**; as thou, Father, *art* in me, and I in thee, that they also may be **one** in us: that the world may believe that thou hast sent me. And the glory which thou gavest me I have given them; that they may be **one**, even as we are **one**: I in them, and thou in me, that they may be made perfect in **one**; and that the world may know that thou hast sent me, and hast loved them, as thou hast loved me."

Jesus said He only says & does what He sees the Father doing

John 5:19 "Then answered Jesus and said unto them, Verily, verily, I say unto you, **The Son can do nothing of himself, but what he seeth the Father do: for what things soever he doeth, these also doeth the Son likewise."**

John 5:30 **"I can of mine own self do nothing: as I hear, I judge: and my judgment is just; because I seek not mine own will, but the will of the Father which hath sent me."**

John 7:16 "Jesus answered them, and said, **My doctrine is not mine, but his that sent me."**

John 12:49 **"For I have not spoken of myself; but the Father which sent me, he gave me a commandment, what I should say, and what I should speak."**

John 12:50 "And I know that his commandment is life everlasting: **whatsoever I speak therefore, even as the Father said unto me, so I speak."**

John 14:10 "Believest thou not that I am in the Father, and the Father in me? **the words that I speak unto you I speak not of myself: but the Father that dwelleth in me, he doeth the works."**

John 14:24 **"He that loveth me not keepeth not my sayings: and the word which ye hear is not mine, but the Father's which sent me."**

Paul said to imitate himself as he imitates Christ

1 Corinthians 4:15–17 "For though ye have ten thousand instructors in Christ, yet have ye not many fathers: for in Christ Jesus I have begotten you through the gospel. Wherefore I beseech you, **be ye followers of me**. For this cause have I sent unto you Timotheus, who is my beloved son, and faithful in the Lord, who shall bring you into remembrance of my ways which be in Christ, as I teach every where in every church."

1 Corinthians 11:1 **"Be ye followers of me, even as I also am of Christ."**

Philippians 3:17 "Brethren, **be followers together of me**, and mark them which walk so as ye have us for an ensample."

Philippians 4:9 "**Those things**, which ye have both **learned**, and **received**, and **heard**, and **seen in me, do**: and the God of peace shall be with you."

2 Timothy 3:10–11 "**But thou hast fully known my doctrine**, manner of life, purpose, faith, longsuffering, charity, patience, persecutions, afflictions, which came unto me at Antioch, at Iconium, at Lystra; what persecutions I endured: but out of them all the Lord delivered me."

2 Timothy 3:15-16 "And that from a child thou hast known the holy scriptures, which are able to make thee wise unto salvation through faith which is in Christ Jesus. All scripture is given by inspiration of God, and is **profitable for doctrine**, for **reproof**, for **correction**, for **instruction in righteousness**:"

It is impossible for the Torah to be profitable for doctrine, reproof, correction, and instruction in righteousness if it has been done away with!

Philippians 3:5 "Circumcised the eighth day, of the stock of Israel, of the tribe of Benjamin, an **Hebrew of the Hebrews**; as touching the law, a Pharisee;"

What was Paul doing?

Paul said to imitate himself as he imitated Jesus. **Paul taught Jesus without the New Testament because it had not been written yet. He only had the Old Testament. Yet, he won people to Messiah!**

Act 28:23 "And when they had appointed him a day, there came many to him into *his* lodging; to whom he expounded and testified the kingdom of God, **persuading them concerning Jesus, both out of the law of Moses, and *out of* the prophets, from morning till evening**."

Jesus taught of Himself using the Tanakh (Old Testament) on the road to Emmaus!

God taught Moses His (**Torah = Teaching, Instruction**) Law. Moses, in turn, taught gentile converts that same (**Torah = Teaching, Instruction**) Law. Jesus taught Moses, and Paul taught Moses. Therefore, Paul taught converted Gentiles the (**Torah = Teaching, Instruction**) Law.

So again, I ask, if you had to, could you lead someone to Jesus just by using the Tanakh (Old Testament)? If not, why not? How many sermons have you heard regarding Jesus in the Tanakh (Old Testament)? Most people I've asked tell me anywhere from none to only a handful. The point I'm trying to make is that we've all been robbed!

The Resume of Apollos

The life of Apollos must also be considered. Apollos is a very informative character in the Bible. Although Apollos is not mentioned much in the Bible, what is said about him concerning Jesus is remarkable yet often overlooked!

Acts 18:24-28 "And a certain Jew named Apollos, born at Alexandria, an eloquent man, *and* **mighty in the scriptures**, came to Ephesus. This man was instructed in the way of the Lord; and being fervent in the spirit, he spake and taught diligently the things of the Lord, knowing only the baptism of John. And he began to speak boldly in the synagogue: whom when Aquila and Priscilla had heard, they took him unto *them,* and expounded unto him the way of God more perfectly. And when he was disposed to pass into Achaia, the brethren wrote, exhorting the disciples to receive him: who, when he was come, helped them much which had believed through grace: **For he mightily convinced the Jews, *and that* publickly, shewing by the scriptures that Jesus was Christ.**"

Here in **Acts 18:24-28**, we see a certain Jew named Apollos, born in Alexandria, **who was mighty in the Scriptures** and **used the Scriptures mightily to convince Jews that Jesus was the Messiah.** One thing that is often overlooked is the use of the word "Scripture" or "Scriptures" in the New Testament. **Every time the word "Scripture" or "Scriptures" is used, it is referring to the Old Testament because the New Testament had not been written yet.**

Apollos was born in Alexandria, Egypt. At that time, Alexandria was the home of many Jews and had one of the largest, if not the largest, libraries in the world. Josephus says the city had a library of over half a million scrolls.

Priscilla and Aquila are inspiring because they gave Apollos the realization of who Jesus really was. Once Apollos realized who Jesus was, **he mightily convinced Jews that Jesus was the Messiah by using the Scriptures, which is the Tanakh (Old Testament).**

Priscilla and Aquila helped to fill in the missing pieces of the Gospel story that Apollos needed as a new Christ follower to be adequately prepared for a powerful preaching ministry. My intention is to help show you some of these missing pieces of our Messiah's story that have been discarded by and large by the mainstream church today! By seeing these pieces, it should help to develop a much deeper level of intimacy with Jesus. **Because once you see it, you can't unsee it!**

Jesus' life was not spent inventing a new religion but in proclaiming the kingdom of God, teaching and healing, and in his sacrificial death ushering in a renewed covenant already promised to Israel in the Hebrew Scriptures **(Jeremiah 31:31-34). In this renewed covenant, God's Torah would be written on people's minds and hearts**, available to us only through the love and sacrifice of the Messiah.

Remember one of my previous questions? Could you lead someone to Jesus just by using the Old Testament? If your answer is no, my question is, why not? If you're unable to lead someone to Jesus just by using the Tanakh (Old Testament), then with all due respect, you are still on milk!

Infants must survive on milk because they are not mature enough to process solid food. Over time, however, as the child's body grows, they need to move on to something other than just milk. They need meat! **Hebrews 5:13-14** "For everyone who partakes *only* of milk *is* unskilled in the word of righteousness, for he is a babe. But solid food belongs to those who are of full age, *that is,* those who by reason of use have their senses exercised to discern both good and evil." Pastor Chris Truby once said, "We have been living off of crumbs while God wants **to have a feast!"** **Jeremiah 15:16** "Your words were found, and I ate them, And Your word was to me the joy and rejoicing of my heart; For I am called by Your name, O LORD God of hosts."

As stated previously, at the time of the writing of this book, there are nearly 50,000 Christian denominations. With that many denominations, it is obvious there are different mindsets at work. People have forgotten who they are and where they came from.

So, how do we become one? We achieve this by reattaching ourselves to the root! Again, as Pastor Scott Stewart says, when you go to the root, you find the fruit! Once you realize who you are in Jesus, the Bible comes alive even more.

As you can see, one of Satan's strategies has been to do away with our Hebraic root, or origin. With that being said, it's crucial to have an understanding of whether covenants are done away with or are still in effect today.

Covenants

There are many covenants in the Bible. However, we are going to examine a few of these covenants briefly. Some of these covenants are looked at as being obsolete or no longer in effect. Often times these covenants are perceived to be "just for the Jews." Also, many times, these covenants are perceived to cancel one another out once another covenant comes along. Religious leaders of the 1st century were caught up in the traditions of man, doing away with the Torah, just like many religious leaders today (**Mark 7:8-13**). They are adding to and taking away. The Jews added to the Word, and the Christians took away from the Word.

Covenant with Noah: God made a covenant with Noah after the flood that He would never again destroy the earth by water! God's promise of the covenant was a rainbow in the sky. **Genesis 9:16** "The rainbow shall be in the cloud, and I will look on it to remember the **everlasting covenant**

between God and every living creature of all flesh that *is* on the earth." That verse tells us that this covenant is **everlasting**! Here we are several thousand years later, and we still see God's beautiful rainbows in the sky.

Covenant with Abraham: God made a covenant with Abraham concerning the land of Israel.

Genesis 13:15 "for all the land which you see I give to you and your descendants **forever**."

Genesis 17:7-8 says, "Yes, I will establish My covenant between Me and you and your seed after you **throughout their generations for an everlasting covenant**, in order to be your God and your seed's God after you. I will give to you and to your seed after you the land where you are an outsider—the whole land of Canaan—as an everlasting possession, and I will be their God."

Genesis 17:13 "He that is born in thy house, and he that is bought with thy money, must needs be circumcised: and my covenant shall be in your flesh for an **everlasting covenant**."

Genesis 17:19 "And God said, Sarah thy wife shall bear thee a son indeed; and thou shalt call his name Isaac: and **I will establish my covenant with him for an everlasting covenant,** *and* **with his seed after him**."

Also, because Abraham obeyed God, all nations of the earth, including you and me, have been blessed!

Genesis 22:18 "And in thy seed shall **all the nations of the earth be blessed**; because thou hast obeyed my voice."

1 Chronicles 16:14-18 "He *is* the LORD our God; his judgments *are* in all the earth. **Be ye mindful always of his covenant**; the word *which* he commanded to a thousand generations; *Even of the covenant* which he made with Abraham, and of his oath unto Isaac; And hath confirmed the same to Jacob for a law, *and* to Israel *for* an **everlasting covenant**, Saying, Unto thee will I give the land of Canaan, the lot of your inheritance;"

Psalms 37:29 "The righteous shall inherit the land, and dwell therein **for ever**."

Psalms 105:8-10 "He hath remembered his covenant **for ever**, the word *which* he commanded to a thousand generations." Which *covenant* he made with Abraham, and his oath unto Isaac; And confirmed the same unto Jacob for a law, *and* to Israel *for* an **everlasting covenant**:"

Concerning the land of Israel, some claim that the land belongs to the Palestinians. The word "Palestinian" derives from the Philistines. For those unaware, Israel was changed to Palestine by Emperor Hadrian in 135. The modern Arabs have adopted the name in an attempt to usurp Israel's connection to the land. What is more interesting is that the word "Philistine" means immigrant. It's not their land it belongs to Israel!

Covenant with Moses: Concerning covenants, the Mosaic covenant is usually the one people have a problem with. However, if you look most of the commands in the Mosaic covenant are a forever covenant; for example, the word "everlasting" pertaining to the commands is mentioned 16 times, "perpetual" is mentioned eight times, "all generations" 9 times, and "forever" is mentioned 26 times. That adds up to 59 times!

Isaiah 40:8 "The grass withereth, the flower fadeth: but the word of our God shall stand **for ever**."

Also, the Bible refers to Mosaic Law as:
"Perfect" - **Psalm 19:7**
"Just" - **Nehemiah 9:13**
"Good" - **Proverbs 4:2**
"Way" – **Malachi 2:8** – **John 14:6** "Jesus saith unto him, I am the **way**, the truth, and the life: no man cometh unto the Father, but by me."
"Truth" - **Psalm 119:142, Psalm 86:11, John 14:6** "Jesus saith unto him, I am the way, the **truth**, and the life: no man cometh unto the Father, but by me." **John 17:17** "Sanctify them through thy **truth**: thy word is **truth**." Jesus is **truth** because He is the **word**!
"Life" - **Proverbs 6:23** – **John 14:6** "Jesus saith unto him, I am the way, the truth, and the **life**: no man cometh unto the Father, but by me." **John 11:25** "Jesus said unto her, I am the resurrection, and the **life**: he that believeth in me, though he were dead, yet shall he live:"
"Light" - Isaiah 8:20
"Freedom" - Psalm 119:45
"Holy" - Romans 7:12

Sabbath

Some people have the common misconception that just because something is not necessarily repeated in the New Testament, then by default, it becomes obsolete. For example, there are some who are convinced that the New Testament does not mention anyone keeping the Sabbath. Therefore, these folks automatically think that the Sabbath is obsolete. Or the classic mainstream mindset, "It was just for the Jews." We don't see "bestiality" by name in the New Testament, even though it's in the Old Testament. Yet any sane person knows that it is an abomination!

Before there were Jews, God created the Sabbath. As a matter of fact, the Sabbath was created for man! **Genesis 2:2-3** "And on the seventh day God ended his work which he had made; and he rested on the seventh day from all his work which he had made. And God blessed the seventh day, and sanctified it: because that in it he had rested from all his work which God created and made." God blessed and sanctified the 7th day of creation for all mankind.

Exodus 31:16-18 "Wherefore the children of Israel shall keep the Sabbath, to observe the Sabbath **throughout their generations, *for* a perpetual covenant**. It *is* a sign between me and the children of Israel **for ever**: for *in* six days the LORD made heaven and earth, and on the seventh day he rested, and was refreshed. And he gave unto Moses, when he had made an end of communing with him upon mount Sinai, two tables of testimony, tables of stone, written with the finger of God."

Leviticus 24:8 Every Sabbath he shall set it in order before the LORD continually, *being taken* from the children of Israel by an **everlasting covenant**.

Isaiah 56:2-3 "Blessed *is* the man *that* doeth this, and the son of man *that* layeth hold on it; that **keepeth the Sabbath** from polluting it, and keepeth his hand from doing any evil. Neither let the son of the **stranger**, that hath joined himself to the LORD, speak, saying, The LORD hath utterly separated me from his people:"

Isaiah 56:6-7 "Also the sons of the **stranger**, that join themselves to the LORD, to serve him, and to love the name of the LORD, to be his servants, **every one that keepeth the Sabbath from polluting it, and taketh hold of my covenant**; Even them will I bring to my holy mountain, and make them joyful in my house of prayer: their burnt offerings and their sacrifices *shall be* accepted upon mine altar; for mine house shall be called an house of prayer for all people."

Sabbath in the Covenant Renewed

One of Jesus' titles is "Son of Man." Therefore, remember earlier that we saw that Jesus only did what He saw the Father doing! **Matthew 12:8** "For the Son of man is Lord even of the **Sabbath day**."

Mark 2:27 And he said unto them, The **sabbath was made for man**, and not man for the **sabbath**:
Mark 2:28 Therefore the Son of man is Lord also of the **sabbath**.

Luke 4:16 "And he came to Nazareth, where he had been brought up: and, **as his custom was, he went into the synagogue on the Sabbath day**, and stood up for to read."

Acts 13:14 "But when they departed from Perga, they came to Antioch in Pisidia, and went into the synagogue on the **Sabbath day**, and sat down."

Acts 13:42-44 "And when the Jews were gone out of the synagogue, the Gentiles besought that these words might be preached to them the next **Sabbath**. Now when the congregation was broken up, many of the Jews and religious proselytes followed Paul and Barnabas: who, speaking to them, persuaded them to continue in the grace of God. And the next **Sabbath** day came almost the whole city together to hear the word of God. The next **Sabbath**, nearly the whole city came to hear the word of God"

Notice that the Gentiles did not ask to be taught that particular day or the next day but to teach them the next Sabbath. The Gentiles understood that the day that was important to the Jewish people was a day called the Sabbath. The Gentiles were not requesting a departure from the Sabbath day; they desired a connection and a continuance of that Hebrew root.

Acts 17:2 "And Paul, **as his manner was**, went in unto them, and three **Sabbath** days reasoned with them out of the scriptures"
Acts 18:4 "And he reasoned in the synagogue **every Sabbath**, and persuaded the Jews and the Greeks."

The Apostles did not abolish the seventh-day Sabbath. In fact, the Book of Acts records that they kept the Sabbath 85 times!

Hebrews 4:8-9 "For if Jesus had given them rest, then would he not afterward have spoken of another day. **There remaineth therefore a rest (Sabbath) to the people of God**."

Most early believers kept the Sabbath until March 7, 321 CE. Roman Emperor Constantine (who was a sun-worshiper) passed a law requiring all to worship on Sunday, the day the pagans worshiped the sun god. Still, many believers kept Saturday as the Sabbath until another law was passed 11 years later. This law forbade it, making it punishable by death to keep the Sabbath.

"On the venerable Day of the sun let the magistrates and people residing in cities rest, and let all workshops be closed. In the country, however, persons engaged in agriculture may freely and lawfully continue their pursuits: because it often happens that another Day is not so suitable for grain sowing or for vine planting: lest by neglecting the proper moment for such operations the bounty of heaven should be lost." History of the Christian Church vol. 2

Chamber's Encyclopedia says this: "Unquestionably the first law, either ecclesiastical or civil, by which the Sabbatical observance of that Day is known to have been ordained, is the edict of Constantine, 321 A.D."

Following this initial legislation, both emperors and Popes in succeeding centuries added other laws to strengthen Sunday observance. What began as a pagan ordinance ended as a Christian regulation. Close on the heels of the Edict of Constantine followed the Catholic Church Council of Laodicea (circa 364 AD): "Christians shall not Judaize and be idle on Saturday (Sabbath), but shall work on that Day: but the Lord's Day, they shall especially honour; and as being Christians, shall, if possible, do no work on that day. If however, they are found Judaizing, they shall be shut out from Christ."

Covenant with David: 2 Samuel 7:9-13 "Wherever I have moved about with all the children of Israel, have I ever spoken a word to anyone from the tribes of Israel, whom I commanded to shepherd My people Israel, saying, 'Why have you not built Me a house of cedar?' " ' Now therefore, thus shall you say to My servant David, 'Thus says the LORD of hosts: "I took you from the sheepfold, from following the sheep, to be ruler over My people, over Israel. And I have been with you wherever you have gone, and have cut off all your enemies from before you, and have made you a great name, like the name of the great men who *are* on the earth. Moreover I will appoint a place for My people Israel, and will plant them, that they may dwell in a place of their own and move no more; nor shall the sons of wickedness oppress them anymore, as previously, since the time that I commanded judges *to be* over My people Israel, and have caused you to rest from all your enemies. Also the LORD tells you that He will make you a house. "When your days are fulfilled and you rest with your fathers, I will set up your seed after you, who will come from your body, and I will establish his kingdom. He shall build a house for My name, and I will establish the throne of his kingdom **forever**."

God promises David that he will make for David a great name. Then God declares that He will give Israel rest from her enemies and that He will make a house for David. God promises that He will establish the kingdom of David's offspring. God also promises that David's offspring will produce the Messiah and build a house for God and that **He will establish David's kingdom forever.**

2 Samuel 23:5 "Although my house *is* not so with God, Yet He has made with me an **everlasting covenant**, Ordered in all *things* and secure. For *this is* all my salvation and all *my* desire; Will He not make *it* increase? "

Jeremiah 33:19-26 "And the word of the LORD came unto Jeremiah, saying, Thus saith the LORD; **If ye can break my covenant of the day, and my covenant of the night, and that there should not be day and night in their season;** *Then* **may also my covenant be broken with David my servant, that he should not have a son to reign upon his throne; and with the Levites the priests, my ministers.** As the host of heaven cannot be numbered, neither the sand of the sea measured: so will I multiply the seed of David my servant, and the Levites that minister unto me. Moreover the word of the LORD came to Jeremiah, saying, Considerest thou not what this people have spoken, saying, The two families which the LORD hath chosen, he hath even cast them off? thus they have despised my people, that they should be no more a nation before them. Thus saith the LORD; **If my covenant *be* not with day and night, *and if* I have not appointed the ordinances of heaven and earth; Then will I cast away the seed of Jacob, and David my servant, *so* that I will not take *any* of his seed *to be* rulers over the seed of Abraham, Isaac, and Jacob**: for I will cause their captivity to return, and have mercy on them."

Covenant Renewed: We explained "Covenant Renewed" in the first chapter; here's a small recap. **Jeremiah 31:31-33** reads, "Behold the days are coming say's Yahweh and I will make with the house of Israel and with the house of Judah a <u>**covenant renewed**</u>." Not according to the covenant that I made with their fathers in the day *that* I took them by the hand to bring them out of the land of Egypt; which my covenant they brake, although I was an husband unto them, saith the LORD: But this *shall be* the covenant that I will make with the house of Israel; After those days, saith the LORD, **I will put my Torah in their inward parts, and write it in their hearts; and will be their God, and they shall be my people.**"

Likewise, **Hebrews 8:8** reads, "Finding fault for with them, He says Behold the days are coming says the Lord and I will ratify with the house of Israel and with the house of Judah a <u>**covenant renewed**</u>." While the Law is forever the same, the administration of God's Law has changed from external tablets of stone to the fleshy tablets of our hearts.[48]

---

[48] Booker, Richard. Torah: Law or Grace . Sounds of the Trumpet, Inc.. Kindle Edition.

There are also over 300 prophecies that Jesus fulfilled, and a list of these prophecies, along with their fulfillment, is available in the Appendix section of this book!

It's Just For The Jews?

Another common misconception is that the (**Torah**) Law was first given at Mount Sinai and was just for the Jews. Since we know that (**Torah**) Law in its original context means **teaching or instructions of God**, it seems silly to think that the teachings and instructions of God are just for the Jews. Especially considering that it teaches us what sin is and protects us from the pitfalls of Satan. However, if you read through the (**Torah**), you will see that there were people involved who were not just Jews. That's right; I will show you how God's plan was initially for everyone all along. Not just the Jews. And it is peppered all throughout the (**Torah**).

Let's take a look at Abraham for a moment. The patriarch Abraham was the first person in the Bible to be called a "Hebrew" (**Gen. 14:13**). All Jews trace their ancestry to Abraham as the father of the Hebrew nation. Accordingly, the Lord proclaimed through his prophet, "Look to the rock from which you were cut ... look to Abraham, your father" (**Isa. 51:1-2**).[49] **Genesis 11** tells us that Abram was from a place called Ur of the Chaldees, which is located in modern-day Iraq, which means Abram was a Gentile! **Genesis 11:28-31** "And Haran died before his father Terah in the land of his nativity, in Ur of the Chaldees. And Abram and Nahor took them wives: the name of Abram's wife *was* Sarai; and the name of Nahor's wife, Milcah, the daughter of Haran, the father of Milcah, and the father of Iscah. But Sarai was barren; she *had* no child. And Terah took Abram his son, and Lot the son of Haran his son's son, and Sarai his daughter in law, his son Abram's wife; and they went forth with them from Ur of the Chaldees, to go into the land of Canaan; and they came unto Haran, and dwelt there."

Genesis 26:5 tells us that Abraham was not only fully aware of God's (**Torah**) Law but that he kept it and followed it as well! **Genesis 26:5** "Because that Abraham obeyed my voice, and kept my charge, my commandments, my statutes, and my **laws**." The English word "**laws**" at the end of the verse here is (תורת), (**Torah**), which is **teaching or instructions of God!** Some English translations have the words "**commands**" or "**instructions**" instead of **law**. However, the meaning is

---

[49] Wilson, Marvin R.. Our Father Abraham: Jewish Roots of the Christian Faith (pp. 3-4). Wm. B. Eerdmans Publishing Co.. Kindle Edition.

still the same. It's (**Torah**)! As you can see here, Abraham kept God's (Torah) several hundred years before the Israelites even made it to Mt. Sinai, and he wasn't a Jew!

Noah was also aware of God's commandments. In **Genesis 6:19-22**, God tells Noah to bring animals by two onto the ark, both male and female. **Genesis 6:19-22** "And of every living thing of all flesh, two of every *sort* shalt thou bring into the ark, to keep *them* alive with thee; they shall be male and female. Of fowls after their kind, and of cattle after their kind, of every creeping thing of the earth after his kind, two of every *sort* shall come unto thee, to keep *them* alive. And take thou unto thee of all food that is eaten, and thou shalt gather *it* to thee; and it shall be for food for thee, and for them. **Thus did Noah; according to all that God commanded him, so did he.**"

In **Genesis 7:1-5**, we see God elaborates a bit more with Noah to not only bring the unclean animals into the ark by two's, but to also bring the clean animals in by sevens. **Genesis 7:1-5** "And the LORD said unto Noah, Come thou and all thy house into the ark; for thee have I seen righteous before me in this generation. Of every clean beast thou shalt take to thee by sevens, the male and his female: and of beasts that *are* not clean by two, the male and his female. Of fowls also of the air by sevens, the male and the female; to keep seed alive upon the face of all the earth. For yet seven days, and I will cause it to rain upon the earth forty days and forty nights, and every living substance that I have made will I destroy from off the face of the earth. **And Noah did according unto all that the LORD commanded him.**" As you can see, Noah was fully aware of what animals were considered clean and unclean. This is interesting, considering we don't get much detail concerning clean and unclean animals until the book of **Leviticus**.

Even Cain and Abel were aware of the **Torah**. **Genesis 4:3-5** "And in process of time it came to pass, that Cain brought of the fruit of the ground an offering unto the LORD. And Abel, he also brought of the firstlings of his flock and of the fat thereof. And the LORD had respect unto Abel and to his offering: But unto Cain and to his offering he had not respect. And Cain was very wroth, and his countenance fell." As you can see, both Cain and Abel gave offerings to the Lord!

The Mixed Multitude

Exodus 12:38 "And a **mixed multitude** went up also with them; and flocks, and herds, *even* very much cattle."

There was a mixed multitude that left Egypt along with the Israelites. As you will see, this mixed multitude were strangers traveling with the Israelites. These strangers were not Hebrews, Jews, or Israelites. They were Gentiles!

Regarding Pesach (Passover): Exodus 12:48-49 "And when a **stranger** shall sojourn with thee, and will keep the passover to the LORD, let all his males be circumcised, and then let him come near and keep it; **and he shall be as one that is born in the land**: for no uncircumcised person shall eat thereof. **The same law applies both to the native-born and to the foreigner residing among you**"

Regarding Shavuot (Pentecost): Deuteronomy 16:11 "And thou shalt rejoice before the LORD thy God, thou, and thy son, and thy daughter, and thy manservant, and thy maidservant, and the Levite that *is* within thy gates, and the **stranger**, and the fatherless, and the widow, that *are* among you, in the place which the LORD thy God hath chosen to place his name there."

Regarding the Sabbath: Exodus 20:10 "But the seventh day *is* the Sabbath of the LORD thy God: *in it* thou shalt not do any work, thou, nor thy son, nor thy daughter, thy manservant, nor thy maidservant, nor thy cattle, nor thy **stranger** that *is* within thy gates:"

Regarding Yom Kippur (Day of Atonement): Leviticus 16:29 "And *this* shall be a statute for ever unto you: *that* in the seventh month, on the tenth *day* of the month, ye shall afflict your souls, and do no work at all, *whether it be* one of your own country, or **a stranger that sojourneth among you**:"

Leviticus 24:22 "Ye shall have one manner of law, **as well for the stranger**, as for one of your own country: for I *am* the LORD your God."

Numbers 9:14 "And if a **stranger** shall sojourn among you, and will keep the passover unto the LORD; according to the ordinance of the passover, and according to the manner thereof, **so shall he do: ye shall have one ordinance, both for the stranger, and for him that was born in the land**."

Numbers 15:14-16 "And if a **stranger** sojourn with you, or whosoever *be* among you in your generations, and will offer an offering made by fire, of a sweet savour unto the LORD; as ye do, so he shall do. **For the assembly, there shall be one statute for you and for the stranger who sojourns with you, a statute forever throughout your generations. You**

and the sojourner shall be alike before the LORD. One law and one rule shall be for you and for the stranger who sojourns with you."

Regarding Sukkot (Tabernacles): Deuteronomy 16:14 " And you shall rejoice in your feast, you and your son and your daughter, your male servant and your female servant and the Levite, the **stranger** and the fatherless and the widow, who *are* within your gates.

Deuteronomy 29:10-15 "Ye stand this day all of you before the LORD your God; your captains of your tribes, your elders, and your officers, *with* all the men of Israel, Your little ones, your wives, **and thy stranger that *is* in thy camp**, from the hewer of thy wood unto the drawer of thy water: **That thou shouldest enter into covenant with the LORD thy God, and into his oath, which the LORD thy God maketh with thee this day: That he may establish thee to day for a people unto himself, and *that* he may be unto thee a God**, as he hath said unto thee, and as he hath sworn unto thy fathers, to Abraham, to Isaac, and to Jacob. Neither with you only do I make this covenant and this oath; But with *him* that standeth here with us this day before the LORD our God, and also with *him* that *is* not here with us this day:"

Deuteronomy 31:10-13 "And Moses commanded them, saying, At the end of *every* seven years, in the solemnity of the year of release, in the feast of tabernacles, When all Israel is come to appear before the LORD thy God in the place which he shall choose, thou shalt read this law before all Israel in their hearing. Gather the people together, men, and women, and children, and thy **stranger** that *is* within thy gates, that they may hear, and that they may learn, and fear the LORD your God, and observe to **do all the words of this law**: And *that* their children, which have not known *any thing,* may hear, and learn to fear the LORD your God, as long as ye live in the land whither ye go over Jordan to possess it."

Laws About Unintentional Sins Regarding Strangers

Numbers 15:22-31 "But if you sin unintentionally, and do not observe all these commandments that the LORD has spoken to Moses, all that the LORD has commanded you by Moses, from the day that the LORD gave commandment, and onward throughout your generations, then if it was done unintentionally without the knowledge of the congregation, all the congregation shall offer one bull from the herd for a burnt offering, a pleasing aroma to the LORD, with its grain offering and its drink offering, according to the rule, and one male goat for a sin offering. And the priest shall make atonement for all the congregation of the people of Israel, and they shall be forgiven, because it was a mistake, and they have brought their

Crossing Over

offering, a food offering to the LORD, and their sin offering before the LORD for their mistake. And all the congregation of the people of Israel shall be forgiven, and the **stranger** who sojourns among them, because the whole population was involved in the mistake. "If one person sins unintentionally, he shall offer a female goat a year old for a sin offering. And the priest shall make atonement before the LORD for the person who makes a mistake, when he sins unintentionally, to make atonement for him, and he shall be forgiven. You shall have one law for him who does anything unintentionally, for him who is native among the people of Israel and for the **stranger** who sojourns among them. But the person who does anything with a high hand, whether he is native or a **sojourner**, reviles the LORD, and that person shall be cut off from among his people. Because he has despised the word of the LORD and has broken his commandment, that person shall be utterly cut off; his iniquity shall be on him."

Remember in **Numbers 13** when God told Moses to send one person from each of the 12 tribes to spy out the land of Canaan? The 12 spies saw that the land was very fertile and good; however, there were giants in the land. Despite the great deliverance that they had already experienced with God, being delivered out of Egypt, 10 out of the 12 spies feared trying to take the land from the Giants.

We see Caleb try to reason with the other spies, pretty much saying the land is ripe for the taking. However, they wanted no part of it. **Numbers 13:30-31** "And Caleb stilled the people before Moses, and said, Let us go up at once, and possess it; for we are well able to overcome it. But the men that went up with him said, We be not able to go up against the people; for they *are* stronger than we."

In **Numbers 14**, we see Joshua and Caleb again trying to reason with the Israelites. However, their stubbornness blinded them so much that they threatened to stone Moses, Aaron, Joshua, and Caleb. **Numbers 14:6-10** "And Joshua the son of Nun, and Caleb the son of Jephunneh, *which were* of them that searched the land, rent their clothes: And they spake unto all the company of the children of Israel, saying, The land, which we passed through to search it, *is* an exceeding good land. If the LORD delight in us, then he will bring us into this land, and give it us; a land which floweth with milk and honey. Only rebel not ye against the LORD, neither fear ye the people of the land; for they *are* bread for us: their defence is departed from them, and the LORD *is* with us: fear them not. But all the congregation bade stone them with stones. And the glory of the LORD appeared in the tabernacle of the congregation before all the children of Israel."

God tells Israel that they will spend the next 40 years in the wilderness because they did not trust God. However, God makes it clear that both Caleb and Joshua will go into the Promised Land **(Numbers 14:24, 30)**.

Caleb is the person I want to draw your attention to; he is another great example of a **GRAFTED IN** Israelite. **Caleb was a Gentile** whose father was a Kenezite (**Joshua 14:6**) of the Canaanites. Caleb's name in Hebrew is (כלב), which means "dog." What's even more amazing is Caleb, being a foreigner **(Gentile)** who was grafted into Judah, and Joshua, a native-born Ephraimite **(Hebrew)**, were the only two people who came out of Egypt, being "SAVED" at the first Passover, that was preserved in the wilderness by God and allowed to **cross over** the Jordan river into the "promised land." **Joshua and Caleb represent Jew and Gentile as one!**

Romans 10:12-13 "For **there is no difference between the Jew and the Greek**: for the same Lord over all is rich unto all that call upon him. For **whosoever shall call upon the name of the Lord shall be saved."**

Galatians 3:7 "Therefore know that *only* those who are of faith are sons of Abraham." **(Referring to those who have faith in God)**

Galatians 3:28 "**There is neither Jew nor Greek, there is neither bond nor free, there is neither male nor female: for ye are all one in Christ Jesus."**

Esther was a Jew who went to the Gentiles. Ruth was a Gentile who went to the Jews. Both Ruth and Rahab were Gentiles who were grafted into Israel long before Paul wrote **Romans 11** and were even included in the lineage of Jesus listed in **Matthew 1:5**

Everything up to this point was written to build a foundation before moving forward so that you can have a better understanding. We have been able to establish an understanding of our Hebraic roots and the covenants that are connected with those roots. We have also established who we are in Jesus and how Jesus desires for us all to be one. Next, we will go to the root to find the fruit!

GO TO THE ROOT TO FIND THE FRUIT

Genesis 11:1 "And the whole earth was of one language, and of one speech."

It's easier to relate to someone if you understand their language. Language is what defines a culture. For instance, if you were dating someone you were in love with, but they spoke a different language than you, and you didn't speak their language, communication would be very tough. Remember in the previous chapter, we discussed having the same mindset as Jesus and being likeminded? Jesus was a Hebrew; therefore, in order to think like a Hebrew, you speak Hebrew. The mind of Christ means thinking like Christ.

1 Corinthians 1:10 "Now I beseech you, brethren, by the name of our Lord Jesus Christ, that ye all speak the same thing, and *that* there be no divisions among you; but *that* ye be perfectly joined together in the same mind and in the same judgment."

1 Corinthians 2:12-16 "Now we have received, not the spirit of the world, but the spirit which is of God; that we might know the things that are freely given to us of God. Which things also we speak, not in the words which man's wisdom teacheth, but which the Holy Ghost teacheth; comparing spiritual things with spiritual. But the natural man receiveth not the things of the Spirit of God: for they are foolishness unto him: neither can he know *them,* because they are spiritually discerned. But he that is spiritual judgeth all things, yet he himself is judged of no man. For who hath known the mind of the Lord, that he may instruct him? But we have the mind of Christ."

The Hebrew Alephbet consists of 22 letters. Hebrew is the most unique language in the world. Each letter has its own name, meaning, and numerical value.

Numerical

Name	Meaning	Value
Aleph א	Ox, Leader, First, Strength, Beginning	1
Bet ב	Tent, House, Household, Family	2
Gimel ג	Camel, Pride, Benefit	3
Dalet ד	Door, Doorway, Path, Enter	4
Hey ה	Window, To Reveal, Behold	5
Vav ו	Nail, Tent Peg, To Secure, Attach	6
Zayin ז	Weapon, To Cutoff, Cut	7
Chet ח	Fence, Hedge, Chamber, Private, Separate	8
Tet ט	To Twist, A Snake, To Surround	9
Yod י	Hand, Closed Hand, To Make, A Deed, Work	10
Khaf כ	Arm, Open Hand, Palm, Cover, Allow, Open	20
Lamed ל	Staff, Teach, Prod, Control, Authority, Cattle Goad	30
Mem מ	Water, Ocean or Sea, Massive, Chaos, Liquid	40
Nun נ	Fish, Activity, Life	50
Samekh ס	To Prop up, Support, Lift Up, Turn	60
Ayin ע	Eye, To See, Know, Experience	70
Pey פ	Mouth, To Speak, Open, A Word	80
Tzaddi צ	Fish Hook, To Draw, Need, Desire, Harvest	90
Qoof ק	Back of the Head, Behind, Last, Least	100
Resh ר	Head, A Person, The highest, The Greatest	200
Shin ש	Teeth, To consume, To Destroy	300
Tav ת	Sign, Mark, Covenant or Seal, Cross	400

As you can see, God included a commentary within each Hebrew letter so that He could speak to us not just corporately but individually! Biblical Hebrew consists of only around 8,000 words. That means that each word has different meanings or expressions.

For instance, imagine you have a 10,000 sqft house, and this house represents the Hebrew language. Now imagine moving from this 10,000 sqft house to a 1,000 sqft house, which represents Greek. Oh, and by the way, you have to take everything with you. After you have moved to the 1,000 sqft house that represents Greek, you then decide to downsize again and move to a 500 sqft house that represents Latin & from there a 250 sqft house that represents English.

Martin Luther said, "The Hebrew language is held of little account because of a lack of dutifulness or perhaps out of despair at its difficulty ... Without this language there can be no understanding of Scripture, for the selfsame New Testament, though written in Greek, is full of Hebraisms. Therefore it has been correctly said: The Jews drink from springs, the Greeks from rivulets, the Romans, from puddles."[50] Something to think about: if Hebrew is the spring, Greek is the stream, and Latin is a pool, then what is English?

Girdlestone's Old Testament Synonyms says, "The Hebrew language, though poor in some respects, e.g. in tenses, is rich in others; and probably no better language could have been selected for the purpose of preparing the way of Messiah."

He points out the variety and richness of the Hebrew language and gives examples, such as seven Hebrew words rendered black in the King James Version: there are eight words translated axe; 12 words for beauty, 12 for body; 14 for dark; 18 are rendered fear; 22 for branch; 26 for cover; 42 for cut; 60 for break; 66 for bring; 74 are rendered take.

It is deplorably obvious that in reading our English translation of the Bible that, we are missing much of the richness and flavor of the original language. The exact shade of meaning is lost when 74 different words in Hebrew appear in English as the single word "take"![51]

Believe it or not, the Greek, Latin, and English alphabets were derived from Hebrew. That's right; the Greek, Latin, and English letters were borrowed from the Hebrew Aleph bet. In other words, Hebrew is the root language of Greek, Latin, and English. As you can see on the following chart, we went from the Aleph Bet to the Alpha Bet!

---

[50] Luther's "Table Talk," Aug 9 1532, as recorded by C. Cordatus
[51] https://www.yaiy.org/literature/HebrewOrigionalLang.html

Alphabet Evolution

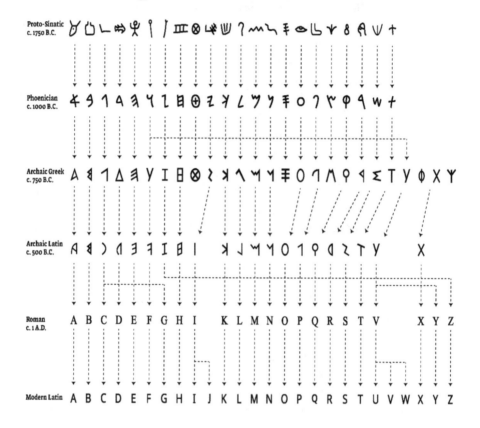

Hebrew was the prototype for Greek. Greek was the prototype for Latin, which was the prototype for German and English, along with all other languages. So, if you go backward, Hebrew becomes the parent language. Hebrew was the language at the Tower of Babel, which was the language of Adam and Eve, which becomes the language of God!

We are told in the book of Ezekiel in two places that Jerusalem is the center of the world. For example, **Ezekiel 5:5** says, "Thus saith the Lord GOD; This *is* Jerusalem: I have set it in the **midst** of the nations and countries *that are* round about her." And again, in **Ezekiel 38:12**, the Jewish people are referred to as the people who live at the "center of the world." And actually, the literal Hebrew reads, "the navel of the world." The Hebrew word "**CENTER**" mentioned in that scripture describing the people "who dwell in the **CENTER** of the land" is (טַבּוּר) "**TABUR**." And while there are different words in the Hebrew language that refer to **CENTER**, such as a structural-center, a conceptual-center, a mathematical-center etc., the word **TABUR's** primary use in Hebrew is referring to the biological-center, the navel, the bellybutton of the human body! Of all the different words that the prophet Ezekiel could have used to convey his epic vision, his perspective of the land of Israel is that it is the "**Navel of the Earth**," or, as others would say, the "**Bellybutton of the planet**."

The bellybutton is where the umbilical cord is connecting the baby to the mother. It is THE LINK that provides and sustains life for the newborn. In the context of Ezekiel's biblical prophecy, that **TABUR** land is the point of connection between heaven and earth; the link through which divine life and revelation flow, carrying out and sustaining God's plan and purpose for His creation.[52]

Jubilees 8:17-19 "three sacred places are located in the territory allotted to Shem. They are the Garden of Eden, Mount Sinai and Mount Zion. These places are depicted as forming the navel of the earth facing one another."

Zechariah 2:8 says that Israel is the Apple of God's eye. "For thus saith the LORD of hosts; After the glory hath he sent me unto the nations which spoiled you: for he that toucheth you toucheth the apple of his eye." The apple of God's eye is Israel, meaning that it is the center of His focus.

---

[52] ***Reuven Doron*** https://www.indiancatholicmatters.org/israel-the-belly-button-of-the-earth/

Interestingly, there is a Medieval 15th-century map called the "Buntings Cloverleaf Map" showing Jerusalem as the center of the earth. What is more interesting is that all languages west of Israel read from left to right, and all languages east of Israel read from right to left. In other words, all languages flow towards Israel. **I believe that this is one of God's ways of showing Hebrew as the root language**.

Since Hebrew is considered the oldest language in the world, which makes sense given that all languages flow towards Israel and that the Greek, Latin, and English letters came from Hebrew. Also, if Hebrew as an identity means crossing over from death to life, if God created Hebrew, and if God and Jesus are one, don't you think it would be odd that Jesus wouldn't speak Hebrew as His native language?

The idea of Jesus speaking Hebrew as His primary language has faced much scrutiny from many biblical scholars. Often, these critics are convinced that Jesus spoke either Aramaic or Greek as His primary language. However, I'm going to show you some examples, Archaeologically, Scripturally, and

Spiritually, why I believe the primary language of Jesus is Hebrew and why I think you should believe so as well. I also want to clarify that I'm not saying that Jesus didn't know other languages, such as Aramaic or Greek; I'm just stating that I believe Jesus spoke Hebrew as His primary language.

Archaeologically

Archaeology is the recovery of man's past by systematically discovering, recording, and studying the surviving material remains that he has left behind. Biblical archaeology is a relatively new science and is approximately 150 years old at the time of the writing of this book. Biblical archaeology has proven and continues to prove to this day that the Bible is historically trustworthy. Over 25,000 Biblical archaeological sites have confirmed and proven the historical narrative of Scripture. Over 100,000 artifacts, cultural items, etc., have been found in Israel and Jerusalem alone. Of the more than 25,000 archaeological sites, along with the over 100,000 artifacts that have been found, nothing has been found that contradicts the Bible.

Rabbinic Literature
Talmud
Rabbinic literature is divided into tannaic works, the teachings of the Tannaim or early sages until approximately 230 C.E., and amoraic works, the teachings of the later sages known as Amoraim. Tannaic literature, except for an occasional individual sentence, was collected and edited in Hebrew.[53] Amoraic works were comprised from approximately 200 C.E. to 500 C.E. The Talmud is a major part of Tannaic literature. The Talmud is a set of books consisting of the Mishna ("repeated study"), the Gemara ("completion"), and certain auxiliary materials. The Mishna is a collection of originally oral laws supplementing scriptural laws. The Gemara is a collection of commentaries on and elaborations of the Mishna, which in "the Talmud" is reproduced in juxtaposition to the Gemara.[54]

The Talmud says: There are four languages which are fitting to be used by all. And they are: Greek for song, Latin for combat, Aramaic for dirges and Hebrew for conversation.[55] This is also said in the Talmud, "In the land of Israel why use Syriac? Let it be either the Holy Language or the Greek

---

[53] Shmuel Safrai, "Literary Languages in the Time of Jesus," Jerusalem Perspective 31 (1991): 3-8 [https://www.jerusalemperspective.com/2563/]
[54] https://www.britannica.com/topic/Talmud
[55] Jerusalem Talmud, Megillah 71b

language."[56]

This, of course, is not a canonical position but merely reflects the depth of feeling against Aramaic among the Jewish scholars. Indeed, the Talmud relates an earlier occasion when Gamaliel – the same Gamaliel under whom Paul had studied (Acts 22:3), and whose astute word concerning the Christians is recorded in Acts 5:34-40 – was sitting on the still-unfinished temple steps. Someone showed him a copy of an Aramaic translation of Job, the first and at that time the only "Targum". So disgusted was he by it, that he told the builder to "bury it under the rubble".[57]

Parables

Jesus used parables in one-third of his teachings. The parable was one of the most common tools of rabbinic instruction from the second century B.C.E. until the close of the amoraic period at the end of the fifth century C.E. Thousands of parables have been preserved in complete or fragmentary form, and are found in all types of literary compositions of the rabbinic period, both halachic and aggadic, early and late. All of the parables are in Hebrew.[58]

Amoraic literature often contains stories in Aramaic, and a parable may be woven into the story; however the parable itself is always in Hebrew.[59] There are instances of popular sayings in Aramaic, but every single parable is in Hebrew.

Dr. Brad Young, one of the leading scholars on Jesus' parables, writes, The purpose of the parables in the Gospels and in rabbinic literature was to instruct. Jesus' parables illustrate and teach, despite the argument of a number of scholars that they were designed to conceal his message from the people.[60] Since all parables are recorded in Hebrew, it would make sense then that when the Bible records Jesus giving a parable, He is speaking those parables not only to His disciples but to crowds as well. This means that those hearing the parables would have understood Hebrew. Also, if the Parables are not found in Aramaic but found only in Hebrew and one-third of Jesus' teachings were Parables, then that shows Jesus spoke Hebrew.

---

[56] Jacob Neusner, "Persia and Rome in Classical Judaism", pg 81
[57] Brent Minge Jesus Spoke Hebrew: Busting the "Aramaic" Myth, p. 16-17.
[58] Shmuel Safrai, "Literary Languages in the Time of Jesus," Jerusalem Perspective 31 (1991): 3-8 [https://www.jerusalemperspective.com/2563/]
[59] See BT Bava Kamma 60^b or BT Sotah 40^a.
[60] Young, Brad H.. The Parables (p. 33). Baker Publishing Group. Kindle Edition.

Prayers

All of the prayers recorded in rabbinic literature, without exception, are in Hebrew. Not one of the early prayers which have survived, whether in a prayer book, in a text discovered in the Cairo Genizah or in tannaic or amoraic literature, contains even a single word that is not Hebrew.[61] There are even statements from the Talmud indicating that one should pray in Hebrew, since the angels of the Lord understand only that language and not Aramaic.[62]

Non-rabbinic Literature

Dead Sea Scrolls

The Dead Sea Scrolls are ancient manuscripts that were discovered between 1947 and 1956 in eleven caves in Qumran, on the northwestern shores of the Dead Sea. They are approximately two thousand years old, dating from the third century B.C.E. to the first century C.E. The Dead Sea Scrolls (DSS) of Qumran are known to date from around the same general period that Jesus lived. More than 25,000 fragments have been discovered to date, revealing an overwhelming preponderance of Hebrew texts. As a matter of fact, approximately 85% of all the Dead Sea Scrolls were written in Hebrew, and 10-15% were Aramaic, but only about 2% were written in Greek.

The Dead Sea Scrolls fall into three major categories: biblical, apocryphal, and sectarian. The biblical manuscripts represent approximately 25% of the Dead Sea Scrolls and are partial or complete copies of every book in the Hebrew Bible except the book of Esther. These represent some of the earliest evidence for the biblical text in the world.

The second major category of the Dead Sea Scrolls is the Apocrypha and Pseudepigrapha, which make up about 5% of the Dead Sea Scrolls. The Apocrypha, which means "hidden books" in Greek, are Jewish books that were not preserved in the Tanakh (Old Testament) but were included in the Latin (Vulgate) and Greek (Septuagint) Old Testaments. The Apocrypha are still regarded as part of the canon of the Roman Catholic and Orthodox churches. Pseudepigrapha, which means "false writings" in Greek, were Jewish writings that were attributed to authors who did not actually write

---

[61] Shmuel Safrai, "Literary Languages in the Time of Jesus," Jerusalem Perspective 31 (1991): 3-8 [https://www.jerusalemperspective.com/2563/].
[62] BT Shabbat 12^b; BT Sotah 33^a.

them. This was widespread in Greco-Roman antiquity in Jewish, Christian, and pagan circles alike. Books were attributed to authors and other characters of the Bible. These include Abraham, Noah, Moses, Adam, Jeremiah, Elijah, Ezekiel, Baruch, and Enoch.

Shmuel Safrai stated, Those works of the Apocrypha and Pseudepigrapha which owe their survival to acceptance by this or that group within the church were originally written in the land of Israel or in the Hellenistic Jewish diaspora, or based upon works written there. Among the works written in the land of Israel are Ben Sira, 1 Maccabees and 4 Ezra (= 2 Esdras). The Letter of Aristeas and 2 Maccabees were written in the diaspora. The works that originated in the land of Israel, at least those which survived in Greek translations or in translations based upon Greek, were originally written in Hebrew.[63]

The fragments of Ben Sira (originally composed about 200 B.C.E.), which were discovered at Masada and Qumran, are in Hebrew. A large part of the book of Ben Sira was found in the Cairo Genizah; apparently reflecting the original version, it also is written in Hebrew.[64] It is possible that some of these works of Apocrypha and Pseudepigrapha had Aramaic versions, and in fact a number of verses from Ben Sira are cited in rabbinic sources in Aramaic, but the original Ben Sira clearly was composed in Hebrew.[65]

The third major category of the Dead Sea Scrolls are the Sectarian manuscripts, which account for the remaining 70% of the Dead Sea Scrolls and reflect a wide variety of literary genres. These include religious-legal writings, liturgical texts, apocalyptic compositions, calendars, and biblical commentaries. Most of the Sectarian sections of the Dead Sea Scrolls are written in Hebrew, showing that Hebrew was a language used daily, not just for religious matters. Scholars have discovered that all commentaries on the Scriptures were written in Hebrew and none in Aramaic. Let's suppose Hebrew was not a commonly spoken language during the second temple period. Why, then, would Scriptural commentaries be written in a language that the majority of people did not understand? The Hebrew found in the Dead Sea Scrolls not only shows but proves that Hebrew was spoken during that time and was very active as an everyday language.

Bar Kokhba

---

[63] Shmuel Safrai, "Literary Languages in the Time of Jesus," Jerusalem Perspective 31 (1991): 3-8 [https://www.jerusalemperspective.com/2563/].
[64] Ibid
[65] Ibid

The Bar Kokhba revolt was a rebellion by the Jews against the Roman Empire. It lasted from (132 C.E. to 135 C.E.) The Bar Kochba Letters proved conclusively that Hebrew was still a living language and was used as the primary means of communication among Jews in Israel a century after Jesus.

Scholars do not divide the letters into Early and Late. They all came from the same period. There were 26 letters uncovered: 2 are in Greek, eight are in Aramaic, three could be either Aramaic or Hebrew (the text is too short too conclude), and 13 are unambiguously Hebrew. These letters are not all religious (some discuss items needed for religious observance) but are of military conquests and other non-religious matters.[66]

Fifteen military letters were found stored in a leather waterskin in Cave 5/6 of Nahal Hever, known as the Cave of the Letters. All of the letters in this bundle were written by men who were involved with the administration of Shim'on b. Kosiba was the leader of the Bar Kokhba Revolt, and most were written in Shim'on's name.

Masada

The siege of Masada lasted from (72 C.E. to 73 C.E.) Masada was one of Herod's fortresses. Likewise, the sixteen texts found at Herod's stronghold of Masada predated the fortress' overthrow in 73. No less than fifteen are definitely in Hebrew[67], with some doubt over the final one.

Josephus (37 C.E – 100 C.E.)

Josephus' references to the "language of the Hebrews" also indicates the Hebrew language was still relevant during the first century. In his introduction to *The Jewish Antiquities* he states: "For it [his book] will embrace our entire ancient history and political constitution, translated from the Hebrew records" (*Antiquities* 1:5). The Hebrew records he refers to are the Bible.[68]

In his discussion of creation and the Sabbath he states: "For which reason we also pass this day in repose from toil and call it Sabbath, a word which

---

[66] https://hermeneutics.stackexchange.com/questions/201/what-language-did-jesus-commonly-speak

[67] Shemaryahu Talmon, "Hebrew written fragments from Masada", DSD 3:2 (1996), 168. Tov, op. cit., 57.

[68] Shmuel Safrai, "Spoken Languages in the Time of Jesus," Jerusalem Perspective 30 (1991): 3-8, 13 [https://www.jerusalemperspective.com/2551/]

in the Hebrew language means 'rest'" (*Antiquities* 1:33). This makes sense only if Hebrew and not Aramaic is intended because in Aramaic the root נ-ו-ח (*n-ū-ḥ*), rather than ש-ב-ת (*sh-b-t*) is used for "to rest."[69]

2 Kings 18:26 tells us that Aramaic and Hebrew are separate languages. The Assyrian general Rabshakeh's advance on Jerusalem and his attempt to persuade the beleaguered inhabitants of the city to surrender. The leaders of Jerusalem requested that he speak Aramaic and "not the language of Judea" so that the rest of the city's inhabitants would not understand (vs. 26). Josephus relates the story in the following manner:

2Kings 18:26 "Then Eliakim the son of Hilkiah, Shebna, and Joah said to *the* Rabshakeh, "Please speak to your servants in Aramaic, for we understand *it;* and do not speak to us in Hebrew in the hearing of the people who *are* on the wall."

As Rabshakeh spoke these words in Hebrew, with which language he was familiar, Eliakim was afraid that the people might overhear them and be thrown into consternation, and he asked him to speak in συριστί [*sūristi*, Syriac, i.e., Aramaic]. (Antiquities of the Jews 10:8)

The language of the Jews and of the Bible is clearly Hebrew according to Josephus, while Aramaic is called Syriac, as is often the case in rabbinic literature.[70]

Josephus in Antiquities 10 1.2 says this: "When Rabshakeh had made this speech in the **Hebrew tongue**, for he was skillful in that language, Eliakim was afraid lest the multitude that heard him should be disturbed; so he desired him to speak in the Syrian tongue." [71] **Josephus clearly distinguishes between Ebraios (Hebrew) and Suristi (Aramaic).**

For those of my own nation freely acknowledge that I far exceed them in the learning belonging to Jews; I have also taken a great deal of pains to obtain the learning of the Greeks, and understand the elements of the Greek language, although I have so long accustomed myself to speak our own tongue, (**Hebrew**) that I cannot pronounce Greek with sufficient exactness;[72]

And being sensible that exhortations are frequently more effectual than arms, he persuaded them to surrender the city, now in a manner already

---

[69] Ibid

[70] Ibid

[71] (Antiquities of the Jews 10:1.2)

[72] (Antiquities of the Jews 20:11. 2)

taken, and thereby to save themselves: and sent Josephus to speak to them in their own language (**Hebrew**). For he imagined they might yield to the persuasion of a countryman of their own.[73]

Upon this Josephus stood in such a place where he might be heard, not by John only, but by many more; and then declared to them what Caesar had given him in charge: and this in the **Hebrew language**.[74]

Josephus (War 5:269-272) points out that Jewish soldiers used a play on words that only make sense in Hebrew. In 272, whenever a stone was on its way (being thrown from ballistea), the watchmen would shout "in their native language, 'The Son Cometh!'" While translators are confused by the Greek text, the answer makes sense in Hebrew. The translator even admits how the words could be confused in Hebrew but not Aramaic. In Hebrew, the watchmen would have shouted Ha-even ba'ah ("the stone is coming!"). However, because of urgency, the words would be clipped to ben ba ("son comes!"). They reduced the syllables due to time constraints. This pun is known in Hebrew and even appears in the NT (Matthew 3:9 and Luke 3:8) "God is able from these avanim [stones] to raise up banim [sons] to Abraham."

This wordplay is unambiguously Hebrew. In Aramaic, the phrase would be kefa ate ("the stone is coming") or the more literary avna ata. Neither sounds like bara ate ("the son is coming"). Another option for Aramaic would be to use the word aven, which is related to the Hebrew. However, aven would change the gender of the verb and still not work to make a pun on "son," bar/a.

Obviously, a warning of dire straits needs to be quick and in the common language. (American soldiers would yell, "INCOMING!" to warn of mortar fire.) That the pun works in Hebrew but not Aramaic means the soldiers spoke in Hebrew.[75]

Temple

While there were a number of Aramaic words and phrases associated with the administration of the Temple and Temple area, the vast majority of references relating to Temple life reflect the use of Hebrew there. The Mishnah preserves many descriptions of various aspects of everyday life in the Temple, including statements of Temple officials which almost always

---

[73] (War 5:9. 2)
[74] (War 6:2. 1)
[75] https://hermeneutics.stackexchange.com/questions/4146/what-arguments-exist-that-would-refute-the-theory-concerning-aramaic-primacy-of

are in Hebrew. Moreover, to date all of the inscriptions found in the Temple area are written in Hebrew, except for two Greek inscriptions, originally part of a balustrade surrounding the inner Temple, which warned Gentiles not to go beyond that point.[76]

Coins

There have been 215 different types of coins found in Israel. Of the 215 coin types found, only one coin was Aramaic, and it was only one side of the coin; the other side of that coin was Hebrew! Ninety-nine of those coins are Hebrew, and the rest are Greek, as Greek was considered the world currency. Coins from the Bar Kochba revolt were also found, and those coins were also in Hebrew.

Church Fathers

In addition to the witnesses of the New Testament (Hebrew syntax in Greek text, Hebrew idiom, literalisms), archaeology, and linguistic scholarship, we also have that of the Church Fathers. Of them, Jean Carmignac says, ``Eight early writers assert that Matthew wrote his Gospel in Hebrew: altogether there are over thirty formal assertions that this was so in the works of Papias, Hegesippus, Irenaeus, Origen, Eusebius of Caesarea, Cyril of Jerusalem, Epiphanius and Jerome"[77]

The most important of these testimonies is that of Papias, a second-century Church father: ``Matthew recorded in the Hebrew language the words [of Jesus], and everyone interpreted them as he was able"[78] `The question of the language in which Jesus primarily communicated to his people also involves the question of which language a biography of Jesus would have been originally recorded. Archaeological data and linguistic research are tipping the scales in favor of Hebrew. A recently published tenth-century Arabic document, which is partially based on an earlier fifth century Aramaic document, identifies the language of `the prophets,' `Christ,' and `the true Gospel' as Hebrew. Furthermore, it excoriates the non-Jewish Christians for discarding Hebrew in favor of foreign languages not spoken

---

[76] Shmuel Safrai, "Spoken Languages in the Time of Jesus," *Jerusalem Perspective* 30 (1991): 3-8, 13 [https://www.jerusalemperspective.com/2551/].

[77] (Jean Carmignac, ``Studies in the Hebrew Background of the Synoptic Gospels," *Annual of the Swedish Theological Institute* 7 (1968-69), p. 88.)

[78] (Grintz, p. 43, quoting Eusebius).

by the Savior"[79]

These are just a few of the archaeological evidences showing that Hebrew as a language was very much alive and well during Jesus's time on earth in the first century. Now, we will move into some of the Scriptural and Spiritual aspects of Hebrew shown in the Bible. This next section will begin to blend the Scriptural and Spiritual aspects of Hebrew, showing Jesus in ways many people have not yet seen!

Scripturally

Of course, the Bible itself is our finest example of an archaeological document. The Bible is full of many Hebraisms that are often missed because, too often, it's looked at through a Western cultural mindset. Once we truly understand that the Bible was written in a Hebrew land, by Hebrews, in a Hebrew culture, about a Hebrew Messiah, it all becomes so much more apparent.

Interestingly, the same individuals who espouse the inerrancy of the Scriptures will take the specific passages in the New Testament that refer to Jesus speaking Hebrew (Acts 26:14) or Paul speaking Hebrew (Acts 21:40), and say, "That means Aramaic and not Hebrew." The "Aramaic Theory" has so heavily influenced biblical scholarship that even those who should be the most capable of working with the biblical text, namely, Bible translators, have translated "Aramaic" when the original text specifically states "Hebrew." For example, The New International Version, published by Zondervan van Bible Publishers, in both of the above-mentioned passages in Acts, purposely translates "Hebrew" as "Aramaic," and only in 26:14 does it even bother to give the footnote "or Hebrew" in italics at the bottom of the page. The New American Standard Bible translates "Hebrew dialect" in both passages but adds the footnote, note, "i.e., Jewish Aramaic."[80]

Aramaic is nowhere mentioned in the New Testament. Even though Greek has a perfectly good word for Aramaic (*Suristi*), the Greek New Testament never once uses it. Instead, the Greek New Testament refers to (Ebraios, Hebrais, Hebraios, Hebraisti, or Hebraikos), which are Greek words for "Hebrew". It is obvious just by looking at these Greek words for the word

---

[79] (``An Introduction to the Research of Robert Lindsey-Part II: Synoptic Theory and Trends in NT Scholarship'' by Joseph Frankovic, *Yavo Digest*, Vol. VII, No. 4, p. 12)
[80] David Bivin;Roy Blizzard Jr.. Understanding the Difficult Words of Jesus: New Insights From a Hebrew Perspective (Kindle Locations 94-100). Kindle Edition.

"Hebrew" that it means Hebrew and not Aramaic. So, when we see some Bible translations that substitute Hebrew for Aramaic, this is a deliberate mistranslation.

There are ten references to the Hebrew language in the NT: τῇ Ἑβραΐδι διαλέκτῳ (*tē hebraidi dialektō*, 'in the Hebrew language'; Acts 21.40; 22.2; 26.14); Ἑβραϊστί (*hebraisti*, 'in Hebrew'; John 5.2; 19.13, 17, 20; 20.16; Rev. 9.11; 16.16). Paul speaks to a crowd in the Temple in Jerusalem "in the Hebrew language" (Acts 21.40; 22.2), and Jesus speaks to Paul "in the Hebrew language" (Acts 26.14). The author of John gives the Greek transliterations of three place names—Bethzatha, Gabbatha, Golgotha—and despite their Aramaic etymology, he accepts these proper nouns as part of the Hebrew language. This author also records that the notice Pilate placed on the cross of Jesus "was written in Hebrew [Ἑβραϊστί (*hebraisti*)], Greek and Latin"; and that Mary addressed the resurrected Jesus in Hebrew as ῥαββουνί (*rabbouni*, 'my master'). The author of Revelation records two Hebrew names: Ἀβαδδών (*Abaddōn*, 'the angel of the bottomless pit' [Hebrew: אבדון *'aḇadōn*, 'destruction']), and Ἁρμαγεδών (*Harmagedōn*, 'mountain of Megiddo' [Hebrew: הר מגידון *har məḡiddōn*]), a place name.[81]

Acts 21:40 "So when he had given him permission, Paul stood on the stairs and motioned with his hand to the people. And when there was a great silence, he spoke to *them* in the **Hebrew language**, saying,"

Acts 22:2 "And when they heard that he spoke to them in the **Hebrew language**, they kept all the more silent. Then he said:"

Acts 26:14 "And when we all had fallen to the ground, I heard a voice speaking to me and saying in the **Hebrew language**, 'Saul, Saul, why are you persecuting Me? *It is* hard for you to kick against the goads."

John 5:2 "Now there is in Jerusalem by the Sheep *Gate* a pool, which is called in **Hebrew**, Bethesda, having five porches."

John 19:13 "When Pilate therefore heard that saying, he brought Jesus out and sat down in the judgment seat in a place that is called *The* Pavement, but in **Hebrew**, Gabbatha."

John 19:17 "And He, bearing His cross, went out to a place called *the Place* of a Skull, which is called in **Hebrew**, Golgotha,"

John 19:20 "Then many of the Jews read this title, for the place where Jesus was crucified was near the city; and it was written in **Hebrew**, Greek, *and*

---

[81] Bivin, David N. "Hebraisms in the New Testament." Encyclopedia of Hebrew Language and Linguistics. Edited by: Geoffrey Khan. Brill Online, 2013. Reference. 01 November 2013

Latin."

John 20:16 "Jesus said to her, "Mary!" She turned and said to Him, **"Rabboni!"** (which is to say, Teacher)."

Revelation 9:11 "And they had as king over them the angel of the bottomless pit, whose name in **Hebrew** *is* Abaddon, but in Greek he has the name Apollyon."

Revelation 16:16 "And they gathered them together to the place called in **Hebrew**, Armageddon."

We've established that the Hebrew language is referenced at least ten times in the New Testament: Jesus, Paul, and Mary speak "in the Hebrew language"; three toponyms bear 'Hebrew' names; even an angel has a 'Hebrew' name. The notice Pilate had placed on Jesus' cross was written 'in Hebrew,' as well as in Greek and Latin. When Paul spoke to the Roman commander, he used Greek **(Acts 21:37)**. Also if you notice at the end of the verse, the commander was surprised that Paul knew Greek. A few verses later, when Paul addressed the people, he spoke to them "in the Hebrew language" **(Acts 21:40)**.

Act 21:37 "And as Paul was to be led into the castle, he said unto the chief captain, May I speak unto thee? Who said, Canst thou speak Greek? The Centurion was surprised that Paul spoke Greek!"

Act 21:40 "And when he had given him licence, Paul stood on the stairs, and beckoned with the hand unto the people. And when there was made a great silence, **he spake unto *them* in the Hebrew tongue**, saying,"

Babylonian Captivity

It is often taught that the Hebrew language was lost during the 70-year Babylonian captivity. "The Hebrews were located geographically in the ancient Middle East, and during most of their long history were under the sovereignty of powers greater than themselves. Yet, remarkably, they were the only one of those peoples to succeed in maintaining themselves through the centuries as a culture. It was primarily their unique religion which sustained them, making them capable of withstanding those forces of absorption and disintegration which would have removed them as a people from the stage of history."[82]

It's very interesting to see that many believe the Israelites lost the Hebrew language and adopted Aramaic under the Babylonian captivity. The Jews

---

[82] Eugene G. Bewkes, et al., The Western Heritage of Faith and Reason, ed. J. Calvin Keene (New York: Harper & Row, 1963), p. 4.

under Moses, who were in captivity for over 400 years, maintained the Hebrew language! (**Psalms 114:1** "When Israel went out of Egypt, the house of Jacob from a people of strange language;") Therefore, why wouldn't they maintain Hebrew in Babylonian captivity? The Babylonian captivity was only 70 years!

Daniel 2:4 Then spake the Chaldeans to the king in Syriack, (**Aramaic**) O king, live for ever: tell thy servants the dream, and we will shew the interpretation.

Ezra 4:7 And in the days of Artaxerxes wrote Bishlam, Mithredath, Tabeel, and the rest of their companions, unto Artaxerxes king of Persia; and the writing of the letter *was* written in the Syrian (**Aramaic**) tongue, and interpreted in the Syrian (Aramaic) tongue.

Esther 8:9 Then were the king's scribes called at that time in the third month, that *is,* the month Sivan, on the three and twentieth *day* thereof; and it was written according to all that Mordecai commanded unto the Jews, and to the lieutenants, and the deputies and rulers of the provinces which *are* from India unto Ethiopia, an hundred twenty and seven provinces, unto every province according to the writing thereof, and unto every people after their language, and to the Jews according to their writing (**Hebrew**), and according to their (**Hebrew**) language.

Nehemiah 13:24 And their children spake half in the speech of Ashdod, and could not speak in the Jews' (**Hebrew**) language, but according to the language of each people.

A composite of these passages, spanning the exile/immediate post exile period, shows the following. While "the Chaldeans spoke... in Aramaic" (**Daniel 2:4**), and the Persians received official communications "in Aramaic" (**Ezra 4:7**), yet "the Jews [spoke] in their own language" (Esther 8:9), ie., "the Jews language" (**Nehemiah 13:24**).[83]

Clearly, just as the Jews under Moses maintained their Hebrew identity in Egypt, among "a people of strange language" (**Psalm 114:1**), so did their posterity under Daniel and Esther, Nehemiah and Ezra in Babylonia, not to mention Ezekiel who, as the prophet of the exile, demonstrably still wrote his book in Hebrew.[84]

Luke 4:17-22 "And He was handed the book of the prophet Isaiah. And when He had opened the book, He found the place where it was written: "THE SPIRIT OF THE LORD IS UPON ME, BECAUSE HE HAS ANOINTED ME TO PREACH THE GOSPEL TO THE POOR; HE HAS

---

[83] Brent Minge Jesus Spoke Hebrew: Busting the "Aramaic" Myth, p. 44.
[84] Ibid

SENT ME TO HEAL THE BROKENHEARTED, TO PROCLAIM LIBERTY TO THE CAPTIVES AND RECOVERY OF SIGHT TO THE BLIND, TO SET AT LIBERTY THOSE WHO ARE OPPRESSED; TO PROCLAIM THE ACCEPTABLE YEAR OF THE LORD. Then He closed the book, and gave *it* back to the attendant and sat down. And the eyes of all who were in the synagogue were fixed on Him. And He began to say to them, "Today this Scripture is fulfilled in your hearing." So all bore witness to Him, and marveled at the gracious words which proceeded out of His mouth. And they said, "Is this not Joseph's son?"

Jesus read a portion of **Isaiah 61**. The book of Isaiah was written in Hebrew, and if Jesus could open it and read it in the Synagogue, it means that He could speak Hebrew and understand it. Not to mention everyone else attending Synagogue. **Luke 4:22** says everyone that was in the Synagogue marveled at the gracious words which came out of His mouth. This means everyone understood what Jesus was saying in Hebrew!

Another example of Jesus using Hebrew is during the Sermon on the Mount found in **Matthew 5:17-18** "Do not think that I came to destroy the Law or the Prophets. I did not come to destroy but to fulfill. For verily I say unto you, Till heaven and earth pass, one **jot** or one **tittle** shall in no wise pass from the law, till all be fulfilled." Remember, in the first chapter, we established the fact that **Matthew 5:17** was a Hebrew idiom. However Matthew 5:18 is what I want to draw your attention too. Notice the words **"jot"** and **"tittle."** The **"jot"** is the English transliteration of the Greek letter **"iota"** and the **"iota"** is a transliteration of the Hebrew letter **"yod."** The **"tittle"** represents the decorative hook on **Hebrew** letters or the stroke of a letter.

Luke 16:17 also says, "And it is easier for heaven and earth to pass away than for one **tittle** of the law to fail."

What else is interesting is that there were anywhere from several hundred, to several thousand people in attendance to the Sermon on the Mount and these. **Matthew 4:25** "Great multitudes followed Him—from Galilee, and *from* Decapolis, Jerusalem, Judea, and beyond the Jordan." **Matthew 5:1** "And seeing the multitudes, He went up on a mountain, and when He was seated His disciples came to Him."

Not only were there a great number of people present, these people understood what Jesus was saying! **Matthew 7:28-29** "And so it was, when Jesus had ended these sayings, that **the people were astonished at His teaching**, for He taught them as one having authority, and not as the scribes." **Matthew 8:1** "When He had come down from the mountain, great multitudes followed Him."

Rabbi

The word **"Rabbi"** originates from the Hebrew, meaning "teacher." There are 13 instances of Jesus being referred to as **"Rabbi"**:
1. **John 1:38** "Jesus turned and saw them following and said to them, "What are you seeking?" And they said to him, **"Rabbi"** (which means Teacher), "where are you staying?" What is interesting about what John did here is that he went out of his way to use the Hebrew term for teacher which is **"Rabbi"**, then proceeded to give the interpretation of what it meant
2. **Matthew 26:25** "Judas, who would betray him, answered, "Is it I, **Rabbi**?" He said to him, "You have said so."
3. **Matthew 26:49** "And he came up to Jesus at once and said, "Greetings, **Rabbi**!" And he kissed him."
4. **Mark 9:5** "And Peter said to Jesus, "**Rabbi**, it is good that we are here. Let us make three tents, one for you and one for Moses and one for Elijah."
5. **Mark 11:21** "And Peter remembered and said to him, "**Rabbi**, look! The fig tree that you cursed has withered."
6. **Mark 14:45** "And when he came, he went up to him at once and said, "**Rabbi**!" And he kissed him."
7. **John 1:49** "Nathanael answered him, "**Rabbi**, you are the Son of God! You are the King of Israel!"
8. **John 3:2** "This man came to Jesus by night and said to him, "**Rabbi**, we know that you are a teacher come from God, for no one can do these signs that you do unless God is with him."
9. **John 3:26** "And they came to John and said to him, "**Rabbi**, he who was with you across the Jordan, to whom you bore witness—look, he is baptizing, and all are going to him."
10. **John 4:31** "Meanwhile the disciples were urging him, saying, "**Rabbi**, eat."
11. **John 6:25** "When they found him on the other side of the sea, they said to him, "**Rabbi**, when did you come here?"
12. **John 9:2** "And his disciples asked him, "**Rabbi**, who sinned, this man or his parents, that he was born blind?"
13. **John 11:8** "The disciples said to him, "**Rabbi**, the Jews were just now seeking to stone you, and are you going there again?"
Also, in Matthew, we see Jesus using the term **Rabbi**:
Matthew 23:7-8 "greetings in the marketplaces, and to be called by men, **'Rabbi, Rabbi.'** But you, do not be called **'Rabbi'**; for One is your Teacher, the Christ, and you are all brethren."

Hosanna

You have probably heard the Hebrew word "Hosanna" before, but do you know what the meaning of the word Hosanna is in Hebrew? The expression Hosanna means "Save Us Please". The term **"Hosanna"** is found six times in the New Testament!

Matthew 21:9 "And the multitudes that went before, and that followed, cried, saying, **Hosanna** to the Son of David: Blessed *is* he that cometh in the name of the Lord; **Hosanna** in the highest."

Matthew 21:15 "And when the chief priests and scribes saw the wonderful things that he did, and the children crying in the temple, and saying, **Hosanna** to the Son of David; they were sore displeased,"

Mark 11:9-10 "And they that went before, and they that followed, cried, saying, **Hosanna**; Blessed *is* he that cometh in the name of the Lord: Blessed *be* the kingdom of our father David, that cometh in the name of the Lord: **Hosanna** in the highest."

John 12:13 "Took branches of palm trees, and went forth to meet him, and cried, **Hosanna**: Blessed *is* the King of Israel that cometh in the name of the Lord."

Amen

We are all familiar with the word **"Amen."** However, were you aware that **"Amen" is a Hebrew word as well? The word "Amen" in a general sense means "to be in agreement." The entire Bible, including the New Testament, is filled with this word**.

Paul concludes with emphatic praise in at least 13 verses:

1. Romans 1:25 "Who changed the truth of God into a lie, and worshipped and served the creature more than the Creator, who is blessed for ever. **Amen.**"

2. Romans 9:5 "Whose *are* the fathers, and of whom as concerning the flesh Christ *came,* who is over all, God blessed for ever. **Amen.**"

3. Romans 11:36 "For of him, and through him, and to him, *are* all things: to whom *be* glory for ever. **Amen.**"

4. Romans 15:33 "Now the God of peace *be* with you all. **Amen.**"

5. Romans 16:24 "The grace of our Lord Jesus Christ *be* with you all. **Amen.**"

6. 1 Corinthians 16:24 "My love *be* with you all in Christ Jesus. **Amen.**"

7. Galatians 1:5 "To whom *be* glory for ever and ever. **Amen.**"

8. Galatians 6:18 "Brethren, the grace of our Lord Jesus Christ *be* with your spirit. **Amen.**"

9. Ephesians 3:21 "Unto him *be* glory in the church by Christ Jesus throughout all ages, world without end. **Amen.**"

10. Philippians 4:20 "Now unto God and our Father *be* glory for ever and ever. **Amen**."

11. 1 Timothy 1:17 "Now unto the King eternal, immortal, invisible, the only wise God, *be* honour and glory for ever and ever. **Amen**."

12. 1 Timothy 6:16 "Who only hath immortality, dwelling in the light which no man can approach unto; whom no man hath seen, nor can see: to whom *be* honour and power everlasting. **Amen**."

13. 2 Timothy 4:18 "And the Lord shall deliver me from every evil work, and will preserve *me* unto his heavenly kingdom: to whom *be* glory for ever and ever. **Amen**."

Paul even tells us in **2 Corinthians 1:20** that by saying **"Amen,"** it gives glory to God! **2 Corinthians 1:20** "For all the promises of God in him *are* yea, and in him **Amen**, unto the glory of God by us."

Also, both 1 Peter and 2 Peter end with "Amen." All four Gospels end with "Amen." The book of Revelation ends with "Amen." Also, "Amen," which is Hebrew, just happens to be the last word in the Bible recorded in the book of Revelation. Ironically, the first and last words of the Bible happen to be **Hebrew**!

THE WORD BECAME FLESH

Spiritually

There are plenty of other examples that can be used, using various aspects of Scripture itself, to show that Hebrew was primarily spoken, but now we will shift to a more Spiritual aspect of Hebrew. This Spiritual aspect will blend in with the Scriptural aspect. This will show the importance that God puts on Hebrew and how **Jesus Himself is Hebrew**.

Hebrew Acrostics

Jesus declared himself in **Revelation 22:13** The Aleph (א) and the Tav (ת), the First and the Last, the Beginning and the End. **John 1:1-3** "In the beginning was the Word. He was with God in the beginning. All things were made through Him, and apart from Him nothing was made that has come into being. The Word was with God, and the Word was God." Likewise, **John 1:14** says, "And the Word became flesh and tabernacled among us. We looked upon His glory, the glory of the one and only from the Father, full of grace and truth." **Psalms 33:6** "By the word of the LORD were the heavens made; and all the host of them by the breath of his mouth."

Many believers of Jesus believe that Jesus is only shown in the New Testament. Due to this way of thinking, believers severely disable themselves by only seeing what is taught in large by a Western-centered mentality. As previously stated, one must realize that we have a book written by Jews about a Jewish culture in a Jewish land, in a Jewish language, about a Jewish Messiah. Therefore, the Old Testament plays just as much of a role as the New Testament.

If then Jesus is the word, every word has letters, and in order to have letters to form words, there must be a language, and every language has an alphabet. The Hebrew language is the most unique language in the world.

The Hebrew language is also the language that every follower of the God of the Bible should learn, or at least try to learn, in order to truly understand what God is trying to communicate to the reader. So much so that it seems the Bible goes out of its way to prove so by using acrostics with the Hebrew alephbet throughout the Tanakh (Old Testament).

An acrostic is a poem in which the initial letters of each successive line form a word, phrase, or pattern. This definition of an acrostic poem seems to be broader than what is normally considered to be acrostic psalms or poems in Biblical Hebrew. In Biblical Hebrew acrostic psalms, poems or passages normally refer to poetic passages that use the Hebrew alphabet as its structure. These Hebrew poems use the letters of the Hebrew alphabet to begin a new line, strophe, unit or paragraph[85].

One of the many interesting rhetorical features of the Hebrew language in the Bible is its' use of alphabetical acrostics. When each successive letter of the alphabet is used, the acrostic is referred to as "abecedarian." Each line begins with a letter of the Hebrew alphabet in alphabetical order.

Acrostics occur in the Bible, in at least three different books in the Old Testament. Those three are the book of Psalms, Proverbs, and Lamentations, where each verse begins with one of the 22 letters of the Hebrew alephbet. It is not known whether there was a special Hebrew name for the acrostic. In a later period it was called a siman ("sign"), and then a hatimah ("signature")[86]. Interestingly, these acrostics appear at least 14 times in the Scriptures!

Even though the acrostic form is generally hidden by other translations from the original Hebrew, it should be proposed that readers are meant to take meaning from it as well as from the text itself. Like most poetry, the text of these acrostics is rich in metaphor, which, when unlocked, can reveal the meaning of the text on various levels. It could also be argued that the very structure of the text, namely the acrostic form, when unlocked, reveals meaning as well.

Scholars have pointed out different reasons why these acrostics exist, such as tools for memorization, mnemonics, and so on. However, considering how frequently these acrostics occur, the importance of the Hebrew language itself is not mentioned! Even the fact that these acrostics were created after the Tower of Babel shows how significant Hebrew really is.

One important aspect to remember is that the Bible was not divided into chapters and verses in the original Hebrew and Greek until many years later.

---

[85] Van der Spuy: Hebrew Alphabetic Acrostics OTE 21/2 (2008), 513-532
[86] Encyclopedia Judaica Volume 2 page 230

Such divisions are entirely artificial in our current translations. However, this becomes even more special because it provides important clues for studying these Hebraic acrostics.

Concerning the book of Lamentations, Chapter 1 has 22 verses, one for each letter in the standard alphabetic order from Aleph (א) to Tav (ת). Chapter 2 has 22 verses, one for each letter. This chapter introduces the curious variation that the order of Ayin (ע) and Pey (פ) is reversed. This same interchange appears also in Chapters 3 and 4. Chapter 3 has 66 verses, three consecutive verses for each letter from Aleph (א) to Tav (ת). Chapter 4 has 22 verses, one for each letter from Aleph (א) to Tav (ת). Chapter 5 has 22 verses, but they are not written alphabetically.

Lamentations is read in synagogue on the fast-day of Tisha B'Av, the ninth day of the Hebrew month Av, which commemorates the anniversary of the destruction of the First Temple. The reason is to recall that God is faithful to His covenant when He brings judgments on His people when His people are unfaithful to that same covenant. Lamentations is considered to be one of the two most tragic books of the Bible. The other is the Book of Job.

Lamentations uses very descriptive language to describe God's treatment of His people. He had strung His bow, stretched out a line over, torn down, cut off, burned, hurled, poured out, destroyed, laid waste, rejected, handed over, swallowed, and broken Jerusalem. Jeremiah wanted everyone to understand that the treacherous events of 586 B.C. were not by any means random. The truth is that God did these terrible things to His own people due to their sins and unrepentance.

In essence, Lamentations covers an almost hell-on-earth-like scenario. It does this by the A to Z, or Aleph (א) to Tav (ת) of emotions, regarding being without God. Jeremiah also shows a foreshadowing of Jesus by suffering even though he is innocent. For example, when he laments about those who are hostile to him "without cause" **(Lamentations 3:52)**. We see how Jesus suffered innocently on the cross for his people. God is just and faithful concerning his covenants. Lamentations show how sin and unrepentance have consequences and lead to being without the presence of God.

After the resurrection on the road to Emmaus, Jesus was walking with some disciples, explaining about himself. **Luke 24:27** Then beginning with Moses and all the Prophets, He explained to them the things written about Himself in all the Scriptures. And then in **Luke 24:44-45,** He said to them,

'These are my words that I spoke to you while I was still with you, that everything written about me in the Law of Moses and the Prophets and the Psalms must be fulfilled.' Then he opened their minds to understand the Scriptures...

The book of Psalms is one of the largest books of the Bible. There is what is referred to as the "Alphabetic Psalms", and there are several of them. Also, considering how many acrostics there are in Psalms, as well as much of the context within the text of the acrostics, it seems like too much to be a coincidence. As a matter of fact, Rabbis say there is no such thing as coincidence.

Psalms 9 and 10 are not individual acrostics, but they actually form a single acrostic. The fact that they belong together is further indicated by their being a single Psalm in the LXX and in Psalm 10, which has no heading in the primary Hebrew manuscripts. These two Psalms were composed together. Psalms 9 runs from Aleph (א) to Kaph (כ) and Psalms 10 from Lamed (ל) to Tav (ת).

The title of Psalm 9 in most modern translations is lost because people aren't reading **Hebrew**. In **Hebrew,** the word "Muthlabben" in the title of the Psalm means "Death of the Son." The Psalms are telling the story of Jesus, and we have every reason to suggest that the death the son of Psalm 9 is referring to, is a shadow of Jesus himself. Psalms 9 and 10 show a picture of the coming salvation through Jesus. While the wicked ignore God, the righteous, on the other hand, seek him out. David rejoices that there is a King who judges with righteousness despite the arrogance of the wicked or the suffering of the righteous.

Concerning Psalm 25, the KJV versification gets out of line with the Alphabet at verse 5, which includes the Hey (ה) and Vav (ו) verses in one. Tav (ת), therefore, appears in verse 21. Also, there are two consecutive verses corresponding to Resh (ר), one of which fills the space usually occupied by Qoof (ק). This Psalm ends in verse 22 with an appended verse beginning with the Pey (פ).

When it comes to Psalm 34, this Psalm follows the standard order with the exception that the verse corresponding to Vav is missing, so the correlation between the verse numbers and the letters is off by one after verse 5. For example, the Tav (ת) verse is Ps 34:21 rather than the expected 22. Likewise, as in Psalm 25, this Psalm ends in verse 22 with an appended verse beginning with the Pey (פ).

The first letter in the Hebrew Alephbet is Aleph (א), the middle letter in the Alephbet is the letter Mem (מ), and the last letter is Tav (ת). When these letters are put together, it spells the word "emet" (אמת), which means truth. **John 14:6** "Jesus saith unto him, I am the way, the truth, and the life:" There you see that Jesus said He is truth! When you look back at Psalms 25 and 34, you see the letters forming the acrostic is somewhat out of order. When you look at the first, middle, and last letters from Psalms 25 and 34, you get Aleph, Lamed, Pey (אלפ), which means "learn"! We need to "learn" about Jesus and his Word.

The next Psalm that has this acrostic feature is chapter 37, which has 40 verses. Most of this Psalm follows a skip pattern with every other verse corresponding to a Hebrew Letter. The first verse starts with Aleph (א), the third with Bet (ב), the fifth with Gimel (ג) and the seventh with Dalet (ד). If this pattern were followed throughout, there would be 44 (2 x 22) verses. But the pattern breaks down in a few places where there is no verse separating the sequential Letters. This first happens with Hey (ה) appearing in verse 8 immediately after Dalet (ד) in verse 7. But then the original plan begins again, with Vav (ו) in verse 10, Zayin (ז) in verse 12, Chet (ח) in verse 14, and so forth until we come to Kaph (כ) in verse 20.

Next is Psalm chapters 111 and 112, in which both chapters only contain ten verses. The whole acrostic Alephbet is represented in standard order from Aleph (א) to Tav (ת) identically in both chapters. The first eight verses each have two clauses beginning with consecutive Letters, and the last two verses have three clauses, so the 10 (8 + 2) verses represent all 22 (8 x 2 + 2 x 3) letters. The clauses will be indicated by letters, such as Psalms 111:1a for the Aleph (א) clause and Psalms 111:10c for the Tav (ת) clause.

Psalm 119 is the most extraordinary alphabetically structured chapter in the Bible. It is also the longest. It consists of 22 sections, each containing eight consecutive verses that begin with the same Hebrew letter, for a total of 176 (8 x 22) verses. The first eight begin with Aleph (א), the next eight with Bet (ב), and the next eight with Gimel (ג) until the alphabet is exhausted. There are no variations from the standard order. Its alphabetic structure is transparent in many Bibles, such as the New International and King James Versions, which present the letter's name at the beginning of each section of eight verses.

Some have said it lacks variety, but that is merely the observation of those who haven't studied it. I have weighed each word and looked at each syllable with extended meditation, and I bear witness that this sacred song has no redundancy in it, but is charmingly varied from beginning to end. Its variety is like that of a kaleidoscope – from a few objects, innumerable variations and combinations are produced. In the kaleidoscope, you look once and see a strangely beautiful form. You shift the glass a little and another shape, equally delicate and beautiful, is displayed before your eyes. It is the same here. What you see is the same, yet never the same. It is the same truth, but it is always placed in a new light or connection, or in some way or other infused with freshness[87].

It affirms that torah will cover every facet of human existence, everything from A to Z. There is no human crisis or issue in which one need go outside the field of torah obedience to live fully...life is reliable and utterly symmetrical when the torah is honored...Obedience to the torah is a source of light, life, joy, delight...The torah is no burden but a mode of joyous existence...The teachers of this psalm are not worried or seduced by legalism. They do not find the commandments restrictive or burdensome[88].
– Message of the Psalms

Concerning Psalm 119:105, it begins with the letter Nun (נ), which means life. Thy word is a lamp unto my feet, and a light unto my path. Jesus said that He is the light of the world. John 8:12 Then spake Jesus again unto them, saying, I am the light of the world: he that followeth me shall not walk in darkness, but shall have the light of life. And again, John 14:6 Jesus saith unto him, I am the way, the truth, and the life: We see Jesus as the light of the world that gives His people life by allowing Him to be a guide through life.

Psalms 119:105 Comments - Note this comment from Frances J. Roberts:

"I shall walk with thee through the valley, and thou shalt fear no shadow. Hold to My promises. They are given to thee as a chart is given to a ship, and a compass to the hunter. Ye may set thy course or find thy way by My promises. They will lead thee and guide thee in places where there is no

---

[87] Spurgeon, Charles H.. The Golden Alphabet (Updated, Annotated): An Exposition of Psalm 119 . Aneko Press. Kindle Edition.
[88] The Message of the Psalms: A Theological Commentary By Walter Brueggemann

trodden path. They will give thee direction and wisdom and will open thine own understanding....My people, heed My words; yea, walk not carelessly; neither lay out thine own paths on which to travel. Ye cannot know what lieth in the distance, nor what adversity ye may encounter tomorrow. So walk closely with Me, that ye may be able to draw quickly upon My aid."[89]

Acrostics from Psalm 119 alone prove the importance of Hebrew because the entire chapter deals with the Torah, which God gave to Moses in His language, which is Hebrew. It all points to Jesus. Since Jesus is the word and those words have letters, this shows that God connected His language to His Torah. So since Jesus is the word made flesh, Jesus is not only Torah, Jesus is Hebrew! John 5:46-47 Jesus is explaining that He is Torah.

Psalm 145 is the last of David's psalms and the last acrostic psalm. This follows the standard order from Aleph (א) to Tav (ת), with the exception that the Nun (נ) verse is missing in some manuscripts. This is why it has 21 rather than the expected 22 verses. In this case, most Hebrew texts lack a verse for Nun (נ), which is why the psalm has only twenty-one verses instead of twenty-two. But one Masoretic text, the Dead Sea Scrolls and the ancient Syriac version supply the words. They appear in the second half of verse 13 in the New International Version: "The LORD is faithful to all his promises and loving toward all he has made."

Proverbs 31:10-31 are the last 22 verses of the chapter. What is interesting is that verse 10 begins with Aleph (א) and continues all the way to Tav (ת); however, verse 10 also begins talking about the virtuous woman. A picture of the perfect bride. Even more fascinating about this particular acrostic is that it is, in essence, showing Jesus as the word (John 1:1). But it also shows a perfect image of Jesus as the bridegroom along with the bride!

If you married a foreign spouse who spoke a different language than yourself, how long would it take before you got completely bored of talking to them through a third person? Probably not long at all! If you want to have a conversation, then you would have to have a translator with you because you have no idea what they are saying. The truth of the matter is that is what has been happening for 2,000 years with the Word of God. We have a beautiful, amazing spouse in the Lord who wants to talk to us; however, we have to go through a third party in order to understand.

---

[89] [109] Frances J. Roberts, Come Away My Beloved (Ojai, California: King's Farspan, Inc., 1973), 16-7

Even though much of what God wants us to see is lost due to translational issues, His love is so vast and infinite that He still lets people see Himself. However, the Bible comes alive even more once we see God's word from His Hebraic perspective. The Hebraic acrostics are almost like a fingerprint of God, authenticating and showing the importance of his language, Hebrew!

Zephaniah 3:8 is a unique verse as it is the only verse found in the Tanach (Old Testament) that contains all the letters of the Hebrew Aleph Bet including the five *sofit* (letters that take a different form when found at the end of a word).

Zephaniah 3:8 "Therefore wait ye upon me, saith the Lord, until the day that I rise up to the prey: for my determination is to gather the nations, that I may assemble the kingdoms, to pour upon them mine indignation, even all my fierce anger: for all the earth shall be devoured with the fire of my jealousy."

What is interesting is that the next verse reads as follows.

Zephaniah 3:9 "For then will I turn (return) to the people a pure language, that they may all call upon the name of the LORD, to serve him with one consent." This language that will be returned to the people is Hebrew!

The Star of David

The Star of David, also known as the "Magen of David," is on the Israeli flag. The star itself is considered to be the Family crest of "David." David's name begins with the Hebrew letter Dalet (ד); however, in David's time, the Hebrew letters were in pictograph form. The letter Dalet at the time closely resembled what we know today as a triangle. Israel took two letter Dalets and turned one △ upside down ▽ and overlaid it upon the other Dalet, thus creating the Star of David. What is really neat about the Star of David is that all of the Hebrew letters are embedded within it!

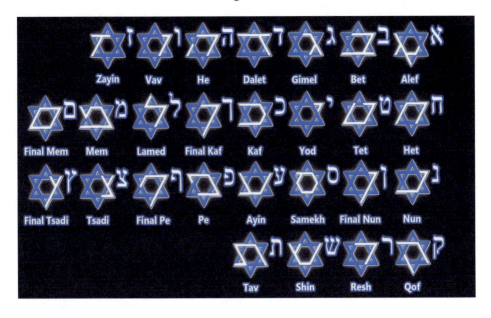

God put His name on his land

The Hebrew letter Shin (ש) is the 21st letter of the Hebrew alphabet. However, it's not just any letter. Shin means teeth, to consume, or destroy In Hebrew, the letter shin by itself is the only letter in the alephbet that is connected to the name of God by itself. The letter shin is associated with one of the names of God. "El Shaddai". Which means "God Almighty". It also stands for "Shalom," the common Jewish greeting that means "perfect peace."

The Shin (ש) is also the letter printed on Mezuzahs that graces the doorposts of every Jewish home. In every Jewish home, there is a Mezuzah beside the doorway. When they leave their home, they touch this Mezuzah and kiss their fingertips. On the Mezuzah is the letter Shin (ש) to represent the name of God, and inside the Mezuzah is a tiny scroll on which is written what is called "The Shema," **Deuteronomy 6:4-9** "Hear O Israel, the Lord our God is One Lord……" When they leave their home, they touch that letter that represents the name of God and kiss their fingertips as a sign of reverence to God and His word. The Shin (ש) is also represented by a hand sign. Most of you will recognize this hand sign as made famous by Spock from Star Trek as the Vulcan greeting. Leonard Nimoy told the directors that he felt that the Vulcans needed some way of greeting, so the director asked what he had in mind, and he held up the Shin (**ש**); the director told him to go with it, and it has stuck ever since. This hand sign is held up at certain times by Jewish priests and rabbis while giving the priestly blessing.

Interestingly, God told David & Solomon that he would put his name on the land, and He backs that statement up in the following seven verses!

1 Kings 11:36 "And to his son I will give one tribe, that My servant David may always have a lamp before Me in Jerusalem, **the city which I have chosen for Myself, to put My name there.**"

1 Kings 14:21 "And Rehoboam the son of Solomon reigned in Judah. Rehoboam *was* forty-one years old when he became king. He reigned seventeen years in Jerusalem, **the city which the LORD had chosen out of all the tribes of Israel, to put His name there.** His mother's name *was* Naamah, an Ammonitess."

2 Kings 21:4 "He also built altars in the house of the LORD, of which the LORD had said, "In Jerusalem, I will put My name.""

2 Kings 21:7 "He even set a carved image of Asherah that he had made, in the house of which the LORD had said to David and to Solomon his son, **"In this house and in Jerusalem, which I have chosen out of all the tribes of Israel, I will put My name forever;**"

2 Chronicles 6:6 "Yet I have chosen Jerusalem, **that My name may be there**, and I have chosen David to be over My people Israel."

2 Chronicles 33:4 "He also built altars in the house of the LORD, of which the LORD had said, **"In Jerusalem shall My name be forever.**""

2 Chronicles 33:7 "He even set a carved image, the idol which he had made, in the house of God, of which God had said to David and to Solomon his son, **"In this house and in Jerusalem, which I have chosen out of all the tribes of Israel, I will put My name forever;**"

Here is a map of ancient Jerusalem:

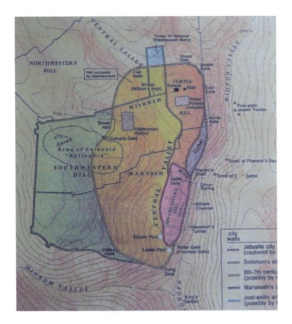

It shows many areas of Jerusalem as they were added through time. Jerusalem sits on a mountain that is surrounded by taller mountains. There are three valleys that come together at the base of Mount Moriah they are the Kidron Valley on the right, the Central Valley in the middle and the Hidden Valley on the left.

Here is the same map with the valleys blackened so you can see them clearly. This is the place where God literally chose to write His name. The valleys here form the first letter of Shaddai God almighty, the letter shin (ש)

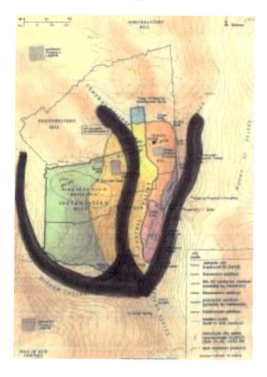

Not only did god embed his name in his land, but His very name is recorded upon our hand. If you hold your right hand out with your palm facing your face, you will see the letters Yod (׳), Shin (ש), Vav (ו), and Ayin(ע), which spells the name Yeshua, which is the Hebrew name for Jesus.

Yeshua

Ayin Vav Shin Yod

ישוע

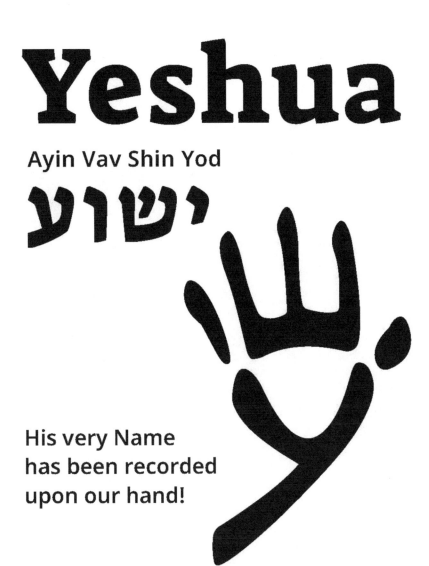

His very Name has been recorded upon our hand!

Put your right palm out and centered over your head.
It is our affirmation of Yeshua's Name and power!

John 3:16 says, "For God so loved the world that He gave His only begotten Son, that whoever believes in Him should not perish but have everlasting life."

For God so loved the world that He not only gave us His only begotten son, not only put His name on His land, not only put His name on our hands, but He also put the letter shin (שׁ), which represents His name, on our hearts.

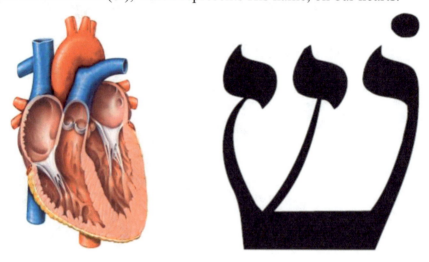

When you cut the human heart in half you can see that God placed his name on our hearts, which just happens to be Hebrew.

What's in a Name?

God paid great attention to Biblical names, as they commonly reveal a person's character, attributes, or destiny. Unfortunately, this is not seen outside of Hebrew because what we see outside of Hebrew concerning names is a transliteration instead of a translation. A transliteration is what a word would sound like, whereas a translation is what a word means.

Matthew 1:23 "BEHOLD, THE VIRGIN SHALL BE WITH CHILD, AND BEAR A SON, AND THEY SHALL CALL HIS NAME IMMANUEL," which is translated, "God with us."

Matthew goes out of his way to tell us that the Hebrew name Immanuel means God with us! God has many names associated with Himself; however, in our English translations, we pretty much just see God, Lord, or Adonai. Once we see these names of God from their Hebraic perspective, we see a much bigger picture of who God is as well as His Character.

English

Hebrew	Transliteration	Meaning
יהוה	YHVH	The All Powerful, Creative Covenant God, He Who Will Be
אל ברית	EL BRIT	God Of The Covenant
האל הקדוש	HA EL HAKODESH	The Holy God
אל סלעי	EL SALI	God Of My Strength God Of My Rock
צור אלהים	ELOHIM TZUR	God Of Rock, The God Who Is My Fortress, Who I Can Run To & Be Saved
אל ראי	EL RO'I	God Who Allows Me To See Him, To Understand & To Know Him Through His Words & Deeds In My Life
אל דעות	EL DE'OT	God Of Knowledge Omniscience
אתי ביום צרתי אל העונה	EL HA'ONEH OTI BEYOM TZARTI	The God Who Answers Me In The Day Of Trouble
אל אמונה	EL EMUNAH	The God Of Faithfulness
אל ישועתי	EL YESHUATI	The God Of My Salvation
אל נשה	EL NASHAH	The God Who Forgives & Forgets
אל חנון	EL CHANUN	Gracious God Full Of Mercy & Forgiveness
אל קנא	EL KANA	The Jealous God

אל צדיק	EL TZADIK	Righteous God
אל שמחת גילי	EL SIMCHAT GILI	God Who Is The Joy Of My Praise Or Exaltation
אל שדי	EL SHADDAI	God Almighty
אלהים קדשים	ELOHIM KEDOSHIM	Holy God
יהוה מקדש	YAHWEH MEKADESH	The God Who Causes Me To Be Holy
אלוה סליחות	ELOHEI SELICHOT	The God Of Forgiveness
אלהי מקרב	ELOHEI MIKAROV	God Who Is Near
יהוה יראה	YAHWEH YIREH	The God Who Sees Everything & Provides Ahead For Me
יהוה נסי	YAHWEH NISI	God Is My Banner Or Miracle, The God Who Leads Me & Sustains Me By His Miracles
יהוה שלום	YAHWEH SHALOM	God Who Is Peace, Wholeness & Completeness
יהוה צדקנו	YAHWEH TZIDKENU	God Who Causes Us To Be Righteous
יהוה שמה	YAHWEH SHAMAH	God Who Is There With Us
יהוה צבאות	YAHWEH TZVA'OT	Lord Of Hosts
רוח אלהים	RUACH ELOHIM	Spirit Of God
יהוה רעה	YAHWEH RA'AH	The Lord My Shepherd
יהוה רפא	YAHWEH RAPHA	The Lord That Heals
אל ישראל	EL YISRAEL	The God Of Israel

אל השמים	EL HA SHAMAYIM	The God Of The Heavens
אל הכבוד	EL HA KAVOD	The God Of Glory, Respect, Or Honor
אל ולם	EL OLAM	The Everlasting God
אל אמת	EL EMET	God Of Truth
אל אחד	EL ECHAD	The One God
אל רחום	EL RACHUM	The God Of Compassion
אל עלינו	EL ELYON	The Most High God
אלהי קדם	ELOHEI KEDEM	The Pre-existent God
אלהים חיים	ELOHIM CHAIYIM	The Living God
אלהי צבאות	ELOHEI TZVA'OT	The God Of Hosts
אלהי משפט	ELOHEI MISHPAT	The God Of Justice
אלהו מרום	ELOHEI MAROM	The God Of Heights
אלהי חסדי	ELOHEI CHASIDI	The God Of My Kindness
אלהי תהלתי	ELOHEI TEHELATI	The God Who Is My Praise
אלהי האלהים	ELOHEI HA ELOHIM	The God Of Gods
אלהי כלבשר	ELOHEI KOL BASAR	The God Of All Flesh
אל שפט	EL SHAPHAT	The God Who Is Judge
אביר	ABIYR	The Mighty One
אל פלט	EL PALAT	The God Who Delivers
אל גבור	EL GIBHOR	The Mighty God

There are 50 names of God listed above, which is an excerpt from Dr. Ron Moseley's book, Spiritually Secure In Just Ten Minutes A Day. Each of these names are in the Bible. As you can see, we have been limited by not sticking with our Hebraic roots. But let's go a little deeper.

Torah Always Points to YHVH

One of the names for God is יהוה, or in English (YHVH), is called the Tetragrammaton. Usually, in our English Bibles, when we see the name "LORD," it's referring to יהוה (YHVH). Earlier, we showed the meaning as "The All-Powerful, Creative Covenant God, He Who Will Be." However, there is another meaning that points to Jesus Himself! The first letter, Y (י), is the Hebrew word for "Yod" or the Hebrew word picture for hand. The next letter is H (ה) or "hey" which means to reveal or behold. Next is the letter V (ו) or "Vav," which happens to be the Hebrew word picture for nail, followed by the letter H (ה) again or "hey," which means again to reveal or behold.

So, if we were to break this down, the name for God or YHVH in the Hebrew word picture would be Y (hand), H (behold), V (nail), H (behold), or "Behold the Hand, **Behold the Nail**"!

Now, let's look at **John 20:25, 27** and see how this is connected with Thomas.

John 20:25 "The other disciples therefore said unto him, We have seen the LORD. But he said unto them, <u>Except I shall see in his hands the print of the nails, and put my finger into the print of the nails</u>, and thrust my hand into his side, I will not believe."

John 20:27 "Then saith he to Thomas, Reach hither thy finger, <u>**and behold my hands**</u>;"

The first five books of the Bible are Genesis, Exodus, Leviticus, Numbers, and Deuteronomy. They are also known as the Torah, which means "teaching" or "instructions."

These first five books of the Bible, as well as all the names of the Old Testament, were originally written in the Hebrew language.

Once we examine the names of these books from a Hebraic perspective, something very interesting is shown.

Genesis: which in Hebrew is called בראשית (Barasheet), means **"In the beginning"**

Exodus: which in Hebrew is called שמות (Shemot), means **"Names"**

Leviticus: which in Hebrew is called ויקרא (Vayikra), means **"To Call Out"**

Numbers: which in Hebrew is called במדבר (Bamidbar), means **"In The Wilderness"**

Deuteronomy: which in Hebrew is called דברים (Devarim), means **"Promises"**

If you take the meaning from the books in the Torah and put them in sentence form, it reveals a pretty remarkable message. **"In the beginning, these are the Names, the Lord Called Out, In The Wilderness and these are his Promises."**

The word Torah תורה is comprised of the Hebrew letters Tav (ת), Vav (ו), Resh (ר), and Hey (ה). Tav (ת) means cross, covenant, or sign of a covenant. Vav (ו) means nail, tent peg, or to secure. Resh (ר) means person, especially the highest person or head. Hey (ה) means reveal at the end of a word; it can also mean what comes from or out of.

If you take the meaning of the letters that spell Torah Tav (ת) Vav (ו) Resh (ר) Hey (ה) and put them in sentence form, it says, **"The Covenant Secured by the Highest Person Revealed."** Or, if read backward, **"Revealing the highest person nailed to a cross."**

If you look at the book of Genesis in the original Hebrew, beginning at the first Tav (ת)

and count every 49 letters after; it spells out Tav (ת), Vav (ו), Resh (ר) and Hey (ה), which spells תורה (Torah). Ironically, if you do the same thing with the book of Exodus, it spells out Torah as well every 49 letters. However, Leviticus does not spell Torah every 49 letters. Instead, it spells out Yod (י) Hey (ה) Vav (ו) Hey (ה), which is Yahweh יהוה (YHVH) every seven letters. Once you get to Numbers, we discover this 49-letter interval works with Hey (ה) Resh (ר) Vav (ו) Tav (ת), which is Torah spelled backward. Interestingly, Torah is also spelled backward every 49 letters with the book of Deuteronomy. So, as you can see, the Torah always points to Yahweh יהוה (YHVH).

Genesis	Exodus	Leviticus	Numbers	Deuteronomy
TORH	TORH	YHWH	HROT	HROT
--->	--->		<---	<---

The Genealogy of Jesus

Remember in John 5:46, Jesus said that Moses wrote of him? **John 5:46** "For if you believed Moses, you would believe Me; for he wrote about Me." Well, believe it or not, Moses wrote the Gospel message. That's right. Moses wrote the Gospel message into the very genealogy of Jesus, which is expressed in Genesis chapter five.

In Genesis chapter five, we see the first ten generations listed from Adam to Noah. I remember reading this as a child, and I always thought it was the most boring chapter in the book of Genesis. After all, it's just a list of names, right? What's the big deal? Remember that in our English Bibles, we have a transliteration of these names, which is what these names sound like in a different language.

Due to this reason, many people reading Genesis chapter five in English or any other language probably skim right over this genealogy since all we see are names and years. However, when we look at these names from their original **Hebraic perspective**, along with their respective meanings, we see something fascinating! Remember that Genesis is a book written over 1400 years before Jesus was born and contains specific information about God's plan to redeem the world by sending his only son, Jesus. Let's take a look at the names in Genesis chapter five.

Hebrew	English Transliteration	Meaning
אדם	Adam	Man
שת	Seth	Appointed
אנוש	Enosh	Mortal
קינן	Kenan	Sorrow
מהללאל	Mahalalel	The Blessed God
ירד	Jared	Shall Come Down
חנוך	Enoch	Teaching
מתושלח	Methuselah	His Death Shall Bring
למך	Lamech	The Despairing
נוח	Noah	Rest or Comfort

When you take the meaning of these names and put them in sentence form, it says: **"Man (is) appointed mortal sorrow; (but) the Blessed God shall come down teaching (that) His death shall bring (the) despairing rest or comfort."** Remarkable, isn't it? We literally have the story of the Gospel of Jesus embedded in Genesis Chapter five. However, the story of the Gospel in the genealogy of Jesus doesn't stop with Genesis 5. It includes the entire genealogy of Jesus!

"Man (is) appointed mortal sorrow; (but) the Blessed God shall come down teaching (that) His death shall bring (the) despairing rest. The fame of Babylon's fortress and sorrow extend like a plant. Beyond the place of division, a friend branches out enraged with fury!

A glorious father, the father of a multitude, laughs as he outwits (his enemy). A mighty prince sees God, (then) joins himself to an assembly, a glorious people (whom) He rescued, stranger(s) in a strange land, captives delivered by God! One who praises the Lord breaks open a way (into) an area surrounded by a wall of great height. O' my people who belong to the prince, a prophet clothed with strength who serves (The Lord) is here! One well-loved, peaceful, and who sets the people free.

My Father is the Lord, the healer of him who the Lord judged and whom the Lord raised up. The Lord took hold (of me), and the Lord is strong! Mighty is the Lord! My strength and help are in the lord! The Lord is perfect! I took hold of the strength of the Lord. It made (me) forget (my misery). Truly (I am) the master builder whom the Lord healed, whom the Lord God raised up, whom the Lord upholds, did uphold and will uphold!

I have asked God about the ransomed of the Lord, the exiles who are in Babylon. My Father is glorious! My God will raise up a helper, the just (one) will the Lord raise up! My God is my praise! God will help! May the gift of Jacob increase (in greatness)! For God is with us."

What you have just read is the meaning of the names put in sentence structure of the entire genealogy of Jesus that is recorded in the Bible! That's right, we literally have the story of the Gospel of Jesus Christ embedded within His own genealogy! However, we only see this in **Hebrew**.

Hebrew	English Transliteration	Meaning
אדם	Adam	Man
שת	Seth	Appointed
אנוש	Enosh	Mortal
קינן	Kenan	Sorrow
מהללאל	Mahalalel	The Blessed God
ירד	Jared	Shall Come Down
חנוך	Enoch	Teaching
מתושלח	Methuselah	His Death Shall Bring
למך	Lamech	The Despairing
נוח	Noah	Rest or Comfort
שם	Shem	The Fame
ארפכשד	Arphaxad	Babylon's Fortress
קינן	Cainan	And Sorrow
שלח	Shelah	Extend Like a Plant
עבר	Eber	Beyond the Place of
פלג	Peleg	Division
רעו	Reu	A Friend
שרוג	Serug	Branches Out
נחור	Nahor	Enraged

תרח	Terah	With Fury
אברם אברהם	Abram Abraham	A Glorious Father, The Father of a Multitude
יצחק	Isaac	Laughs
יעקב ישראל	Jacob Israel	As He Outwits (His Enemy) A Mighty prince Sees God
לוי	Levi	(Then) Joins Himself To
קהה	Kohath	An Assembly
עמרם	Amram	A Glorious People
משה	Moses	(Whom) He Rescued
גרשום	Gershom	Stranger(s) in a Strange Land
שביאל	Shebuel	Captives Delivered By God
יהודה	Judah	One who Praises the Lord
פרץ	Perez	Breaks Open a Way (Into)
חצרון	Hezron	An Area Surrounded By a Wall
רם	Ram	Of Great Height
עמינדב	Amminadab	O' My People Who Belong To The Prince
נחשון	Nashon	A Prophet
שלמה	Salmon	Clothed

בעז	Boaz	With Strength
עובד	Obed	Who Serves (The Lord)
ישי	Jesse	Is Here
דוד	David	One Well Loved
שלמה	Solomon	Peaceful
רחבעם	Rehoboam	And Who Sets The People Free
אביה	Abijah	My Father Is The Lord
אסא	Asa	The Healer of
יהושפט	Jehoshaphat	Him Who The Lord Judged
יהורם	Jehoram	And Whom The Lord Raised Up
אחזיה	Ahaziah	The Lord Took Hold of Me
יואש	Joash	And The Lord Is Strong
אמציה	Amaziah	Mighty Is The Lord
עזיה עזריה	Uzziah Azariah	My Strength and Help Are in The Lord
יותם	Jotham	The Lord Is Perfect
אחז	Ahaz	I Took Hold Of
חזקיה	Hezekiah	The Strength Of The Lord
מנשה	Manasseh	It Made (Me) Forget (My Misery)
אמון	Amon	Truly (I am) The Master Builder

יאשיהו	Josiah	Whom The Lord Healed
יהויכין אליקים	Jehoiachin Eliakim	Whom The Lord God Raised Up
יכניה	Jeconiah	Whom The Lord Upholds
כניהו יהויכין	Coniah Jehoiachin	Did Uphold And Will Uphold
שאלתיאל	Shealtiel	I Have Asked God About
פדיה	Pedaiah	The Ransomed Of The Lord
זרבבל	Zerubbabel	The Exiles Who Are in Babylon
אביהוד	Abiud	My Father is Glorious
אליקים	Eliakim	My God Will Raise Up
עזור	Azor	A Helper
צדוק	Zadok	The Just (One)
אקים	Akim	Will The Lord Raise up
אליעוד	Eliud	My God Is My Praise
מתן	Matthan	May The Gift Of
יעקב	Jacob	Jacob
יוסף	Joseph	Increase (In Greatness)
עמנואר ישוע	Immanuel Jesus	For God Is With Us Salvation

The 12 Tribes of Israel

We have established that in Hebrew, the names given to children have significant meaning. Therefore, it should be no surprise that the 12 sons of Jacob, who became the 12 tribes of Israel, are no different. In the book of Genesis, we find the meanings of the names of the 12 tribes listed in Revelation chapter seven. Here, they are listed in order of birth, along with their meanings.

1. **Reuben - Genesis 29:32** "surely looked on my affliction. Now therefore, my husband will love me."

2. **Simeon - Genesis 29:33** "Because the LORD has heard... He has therefore given me this *son* also."

3. **Levi - Genesis 29:34** "Now this time my husband will become attached to me." It should be noted that God is called Israel's husband in Isaiah 54:5!

4. **Judah - Genesis 29:35** "Now I will praise the LORD."

It should also be noted that "**Dan**" is omitted in Revelation chapter 7!

5. **Naphtali - Genesis 30:8** "With great wrestlings... I have prevailed."

6. **Gad - Genesis 30:11** "A troop comes!" (Gad in Hebrew means "good fortune")

7. **Asher - Genesis 30:13** "I am happy... call me blessed."

8. **Issachar - Genesis 30:18** "God has given me my wages"

9. **Zebulun - Genesis 30:20** "Now my husband will dwell with me"

10. **Joseph - Genesis 30:24** "The LORD shall add"

11. **Benjamin - Genesis 35:18** "his father called him Benjamin." (Benjamin in Hebrew means "the Son of the right hand")

12. **Manasseh - Genesis 41:51** "For God has made me forget all

my toil…"

Let's now rearrange the names in the order in which they are listed in **Revelation 7:5-8** with the meaning next to each name.

Judah: Praise the Lord
Reuben: He has looked on my affliction
Gad: good fortune comes
Asher: happy and blessed am I
Naphtali: my wrestling
Manasseh: has made me forget my sorrow
Simeon: God hears me
Levi: has joined me
Issachar: rewarded me
Zebulun: exalted me
Joseph: adding to me
Benjamin: the son of His right hand.

Now, let's string together the meaning of the names and read the message:

"Praise the Lord. He has looked on my affliction (and) good fortune comes. Happy and blessed am I. My wrestling has made me forget my sorrow. God hears me, has joined me, rewarded me, exalted me (by) adding to me the son of His right hand."

It is absolutely amazing that we see another explanation of Jesus embedded within the names of the twelve tribes of Israel. It's pretty awesome to see what God has done to show us His Son, Jesus, just by using names. Let's move on to our last section

The First and the Last

Isaiah 41:4 "Who has performed and done *it,* Calling the generations from the beginning? I, the LORD, am the first; And with the last I *am* He."

Isaiah 44:6 "Thus says the LORD, the King of Israel, And his Redeemer, the LORD of hosts: 'I *am* the First and I *am* the Last; Besides Me *there is* no God."

Isaiah 46:10 "Declaring the end from the beginning, And from ancient times *things* that are not *yet* done, Saying, My counsel shall stand, And I will do all My pleasure"

Jesus actually refers to himself three times as the beginning & the end in the book of Revelation!

Revelation 1:8 "I am the Alpha and the Omega, *the* Beginning and *the* End," says the Lord, "who is and who was and who is to come, the Almighty."

Revelation 21:6 And He said to me, "It is done! I am the Alpha and the

Omega, the Beginning and the End. I will give of the fountain of the water of life freely to him who thirsts."

Revelation 22:13 "I am the Alpha and the Omega, *the* Beginning and *the* End, the First and the Last."

So, If God is declaring the end from the beginning (Isaiah 46:10, "Declaring the end from the beginning…"), then we have to look at the beginning. We have to look at the Tanakh (Old Testament) to get an accurate picture. In fact, John even tells us to go to the beginning.

John 1:1-3 and **John 1:14**. **John 1:1-3** "**In the beginning was the Word, and the Word was with God, and the Word was God**. He was in the beginning with God. All things were made through Him, and without Him nothing was made that was made." **John 1:14** "**And the Word was made flesh, and dwelt among us**, (and we beheld his glory, the glory as of the only begotten of the Father,) full of grace and truth."

Luke 24:27 "**And beginning at Moses** and all the prophets, **he expounded unto them in all the scriptures the things concerning himself.**" And then **Luke 24:44-45** "And he said unto them, These *are* the words which I spake unto you, while I was yet with you, that all things must be fulfilled, which were written in the law of Moses, and *in* the prophets, and *in* the psalms, concerning me. **Then opened He their understanding, that they might understand the scriptures**"

John 5:39 "**You search the Scriptures**, for in them you think you have eternal life; **and these are they which testify of Me.**"

The first book of the Bible is the book of Genesis which in **Hebrew** is called בראשית (Barasheet) means **"In the beginning"**! We have seen the story of the Gospel of Jesus embedded within the first ten generations from Adam to Noah in Genesis chapter five. Let's see what we can find by going back even farther.

Genesis 1:1 "In the beginning **God** created the heavens and the earth."
Genesis 1:2 "The earth was without form, and void; and darkness *was* on the face of the deep. And the **Spirit** of God was hovering over the face of the waters.
Genesis 1:3 "Then God said, **"Let there be light"; and there was light."**
Within the first three verses of the Bible, you have the Trinity! Verse one, you have **God**. Verse two, you have the **Holy Spirit**. And verse three,

you have **Jesus**! What else is interesting is that the first time God speaks in the Bible, **He is referring to Jesus**!

John 8:12 Then Jesus spoke to them again, saying, "I am the light of the world. He who follows Me shall not walk in darkness, but have the light of life."

John 9:5 "As long as I am in the world, I am the light of the world."

Aleph Tav

Let's take a look at **Genesis 1:1,** which states, "In the beginning God created the heaven and the earth."

That's how we see it in English. However, in Hebrew, we see it as:

בראשית ברא אלהים את השמים ואת הארץ

There are seven Hebrew words in Genesis 1:1, but only six get translated. Remember, the first letter of the Hebrew Aleph-bet is **"Aleph" (א)**, and the last letter is **"Tav" (ת)**. Aleph and Tav together form the word "et," which has no English meaning assigned to it and is not pronounced in Hebrew. You can see the Aleph Tav **(את)** together in the middle of the verse!

Remember, each letter in Hebrew has a unique meaning. **The "Aleph" (א)** represents an Ox head, strength, or leader. The **"Tav" (ת)** represents cross, covenant, or sign of a covenant. The English counterpart to **Aleph Tav** is like the A to Z in English. Likewise, the Greek counterpart is Alpha and Omega.

The letters Aleph and Tav **(את)** literally give their meaning as **"the strength of the covenant."**

Remember what I said earlier? "If Jesus is the word, every word has letters, and in order for letters to form words, there must be a language, and every language has an alphabet." Now, these verses make sense!

John 1:1 "In the beginning was the Word, and the Word was with God, and the Word was God."

John 1:14 "And the Word was made flesh, and dwelt among us, (and we beheld his glory, the glory as of the only begotten of the Father,) full of grace and truth."

Also, **Revelation 19:13** "He *was* clothed with a robe dipped in blood, and **His name is called The Word of God."**

Crossing Over

The Aleph Tav (**את**) is another one of **God's Hebrew fingerprints**, or **Hebrew signatures for Jesus in the Bible**. However, we don't see this in English. What is astonishing about the Aleph Tav (**את**) is that it literally points to Jesus. Listed below are just a few of the over **6,000** examples of the Aleph Tav (**את**) in Scripture!

Deuteronomy 6:5 ‎ואהבת (את) יהוה אלהיך בכל-לבבך ובכל-נפשך ובכל מאדך:

Deuteronomy 6:5 "You shall love *(את)* the LORD your God with all your heart, with all your soul, and with all your strength."

Deuteronomy 18:18

‎נביא אקים להם מקרב אחיהם כמוך ונתתי דברי בפיו ודבר אליהם (את) כל-אשר אצונו:

Deuteronomy 18:18 "I will raise up for them a Prophet like you from among their brethren, and will put My words in His mouth, and He shall speak to them *(את)* all that I command Him."

Deuteronomy 18:20

‎אך הנביא אשר יזיד לדבר דבר בשמי (את) אשר לא-צויתיו לדבר ואשר ידבר בשם אלהים אחרים ומת הנביא ההוא:

Deuteronomy 18:20 "But the prophet who presumes to speak a word in My name, *(את)* which I have not commanded him to speak, or who speaks in the name of other gods, that prophet shall die."

Isaiah 53:6

‎כלנו כצאן תעינו איש לדרכו פנינו ויהוה הפגיע בו (את) עון כלנו:

Isaiah 53:6 "All we like sheep have gone astray; We have turned, every one, to his own way; And the LORD has laid on Him **(את)** the iniquity of us all."

Zechariah 12:10

‎ושפכתי על-בית דויד ועל יושב ירושלם רוח חן ותחנונים והביטו אלי (את) אשר-דקרו וספדו עליו כמספד על-היחיד והמר עליו כהמר על-הבכור

Zechariah 12:10 "And I will pour on the house of David and on the inhabitants of Jerusalem the Spirit of grace and supplication; then they will look on Me *(את)* **whom** they pierced. Yes, they will mourn for Him as one mourns for *his* only *son,* and grieve for Him as one grieves for a firstborn."

Zechariah 11:12

דלו ואמר אליהם אם־טוב בעיניכם הבו שכרי ואם־ל(**א ת**)
וישקלו את־שכרי שלשים כסף:

Zechariah 11:12

Then I said to them, "If it is agreeable to you, give *me* my wages; and if not, refrain." So they weighed out for my **(את) wages** thirty *pieces* of silver.

As you can see, the **(את) is** quite remarkable and clearly shows Jesus, The Word, in the examples shown. But as I said, the **(את) appears** well over 6,000 times in the Scriptures. We've found Jesus in the first verse of the Bible; however, I want to take you a little deeper. Remember, Jesus said He is the first and the last, so let's look at the first word of the Bible.

Barasheet

The first word in the Bible in the book of Genesis in **Hebrew** is called בראשית (Barasheet), which means **"In the beginning"** when translated to English! It consists of the following **Hebrew** letters. Bet (ב) Resh (ר) Aleph (א) Shin (ש) Yod (י) Tav (ת). Once these letters are put together in sentence form, it reveals something truly amazing! Let's look at the letters that make up the word Barasheet. Feel free to look back at the Hebrew Alephbet chart for the letters and their meanings.

The first letter is Bet (ב), which means Tent, House, Household, and Family. The next letter is Resh (ר), which means Head, A Person, The highest, The Greatest. When you put בר together, we get the word "Son."

The next letter is Aleph (א), which means Ox, Leader, First, Strength, Beginning. When you put together ברא, it means to create, or it can also mean "Son of God." Next, we have the letter Shin (ש), which means

Teeth, To consume, To Destroy. Next, we have the letter Yod (י), which means Hand, Closed Hand, To Make, A Deed, or Work. Finally, we have the letter Tav (ת), which means Sign, Mark, Covenant, or Seal Cross.

When you put together the meaning of each letter in sentence form, it reveals an amazing revelation. **"Son of God will be Destroyed with his Hands on a Cross."** As you can see, Jesus is literally in the first word of the Bible!

Regarding the beginning and the end and the first and the last, I have one more nugget that I want to share with you. The first word of the Bible is a Hebrew word called Barasheet, which begins with the Hebrew letter Bet (ב). The last word of the Bible ends with the Hebrew word Amen, which ends with the letter Nun (נ). These two Hebrew letters (בנ) form the Hebrew word **"ben," which is another word translated as "Son."** So literally, the entire "volume of the book" is all about the Son!

Psalms 40:7 Then I said, "Behold, I come; In the scroll of the book *it is* written of me.

Hebrews 10:7 THEN I SAID, 'BEHOLD, I HAVE COME—IN THE VOLUME OF THE BOOK IT IS WRITTEN OF ME—TO DO YOUR WILL, O GOD.' "

I want to thank each and every one of you who took the time to read this book. It was truly an honor to be able to put together something that was designed by God. My hope and prayer for you is that the information you found in this book will give you a renewed hunger to have a deeper, more intimate relationship with Jesus. There are so many people that are starving for the truth. Therefore, I encourage you to take your time gleaning the information in this book, and please remember, this book just barely scratched the surface. I hope you enjoyed going on this adventure of crossing over!

If you're reading this and have not accepted Jesus as your Lord and Savior, or if you're not as close to God as you want to be, now is the perfect time to "cross over." God loves you so much!
I have a prayer that I want to share with you that has greatly enriched my life and drawn me closer to Jesus! It's an acronym of the word **"Trust"**!

T.R.U.S.T.
T – THANKS
R – REVELATION & RENEW
U – USE ME FOR YOUR GLORY
S- STRENGTH
T – TEACH & TALK TO ME

Lord, I **Trust** you! I Thank You for all your blessings upon my life. I Thank You for all You have done, and I Thank You for all that You are currently doing and continue to do for me. Lord, I pray that You would continue to give me **Revelation of Jesus** & please continue to **Renew my mind**! Please **Use me as a vessel for Your glory, not mine**. Strengthen me, Lord, with your Strength, Wisdom, Knowledge, Truth, Love, Understanding, Courage, **and Boldness**! Please continue to **Teach me** Your ways & continue to **Talk to me**. Lord, I TRUST You and love You! I pray these things in Jesus' name. Amen!

APPENDIX

355 Prophecies that Jesus fulfilled

Scripture	Prophecy	Fulfilment
1. Gen. 3:15	Seed of a woman (virgin birth)	Galatians 4:4-5, Matthew 1:18
2. Gen. 3:15	He will bruise Satan's head	Hebrews 2:14, 1John 3:8
3. Gen. 3:15	Christ's heel would be bruised with nails on the cross	Matthew 27:35, Luke 24:39-40
4. Gen. 5:24	The bodily ascension to heaven illustrated	Mark 16:19, Rev. 12:5
5. Gen. 9:26, 27	The God of Shem will be the Son of Shem	Luke 3:23-36
6. Gen. 12:3	Seed of Abraham will bless all nations	Galatians 3:8, Acts 3:25, 26
7. Gen. 12:7	The Promise made to Abraham's Seed	Galatians 3:16
8. Gen. 14:18	A priest after the order of Melchizedek	Hebrews 6:20
9. Gen. 14:18	King of Peace and Righteousness	Hebrews 7:2
10. Gen. 14:18	The Last Supper foreshadowed	Matthew 26:26-29
11. Gen. 17:19	Seed of Isaac (Gen. 21:12)	Romans 9:7
12. Gen. 22:8	The Lamb of God promised	John 1:29
13. Gen. 22:18	As Isaac's seed, will bless all nations	Galatians 3:16
14. Gen. 26:2-5	The Seed of Isaac promised as the Redeemer	Hebrews 11:18

15.	Gen. 28:12	The Bridge to heaven	John 1:51
16.	Gen. 28:14	The Seed of Jacob	Luke 3:34
17.	Gen. 49:10	The time of His coming	Luke 2:1-7; Galatians 4:4
18.	Gen. 49:10	The Seed of Judah	Luke 3:33
19.	Gen. 49:10	Called Shiloh or One Sent	John 17:3
20.	Gen. 49:10	Messiah to come before Judah lost identity	John 11:47-52
21.	Gen. 49:10	Unto Him shall the obedience of the people be	John 10:16
22.	Ex. 3:13-15	The Great "I AM"	John 4:26, 8:58
23.	Ex. 12:3-6	The Lamb presented to Israel 4 days before Passover	Mark 11:7-11
24.	Ex. 12:5	A Lamb without blemish	Hebrews 9:14; 1Peter 1:19
25.	Ex. 12:13	The blood of the Lamb saves from wrath	Romans 5:8
26.	Ex. 12:21-27	Christ is our Passover	1Corinthians 5:7
27.	Ex. 12:46	Not a bone of the Lamb to be broken	John 19:31-36
28.	Ex. 15:2	His exaltation predicted as Yeshua	Acts 7:55, 56
29.	Ex. 15:11	His Character-Holiness	Luke 1:35; Acts 4:27
30.	Ex. 17:6	The Spiritual Rock of Israel	1Corinthians 10:4
31.	Ex. 33:19	His Character-Merciful	Luke 1:72
32.	Lev. 1:2-9	His sacrifice a sweet smelling savor unto God	Ephesians 5:2
33.	Lev. 14:11	The leper cleansed-Sign to priesthood	Luke 5:12-14; Acts 6:7
34.	Lev. 16:15-17	Prefigures Christ's once-for-all death	Hebrews 9:7-14
35.	Lev. 16:27	Suffering outside the Camp	Matthew 27:33; Heb. 13:11, 12

#	Reference	Description	NT Reference
36.	Lev. 17:11	The Blood-the life of the flesh	Matthew 26:28; Mark 10:45
37.	Lev. 17:11	It is the blood that makes atonement	Rom. 3:23-24; 1John 1:7
38.	Lev. 23:36-37	The Drink-offering: "If any man thirst"	John 7:37
39.	Num. 9:12	Not a bone of Him broken	John 19:31-36
40.	Num. 21:9	The serpent on a pole-Christ lifted up	John 3:14-18, 12:32
41.	Num. 24:17	Time: "I shall see him, but not now."	John 1:14; Galatians 4:4
42.	Deut. 18:15	"This is of a truth that prophet."	John 6:14
43.	Deut. 18:15-16	"Had ye believed Moses, ye would believe me."	John 5:45-47
44.	Deut. 18:18	Sent by the Father to speak His word	John 8:28, 29
45.	Deut. 18:19	Whoever will not hear must bear his sin	Acts 3:22-23
46.	Deut. 21:23	Cursed is he that hangs on a tree	Galatians 3:10-13
47.	Joshua 5:14-15	The Captain of our salvation	Hebrews 2:10
48.	Ruth 4:4-10	Christ, our kinsman, has redeemed us	Ephesians 1:3-7
49.	1 Sam. 2:35	A Faithful Priest	Heb. 2:17, 3:1-3, 6, 7:24-25
50.	1 Sam. 2:10	Shall be an anointed King to the Lord	Mt. 28:18, John 12:15
51.	2 Sam. 7:12	David's Seed	Matthew 1:1
52.	2 Sam. 7:13	His Kingdom is everlasting	2Peter 1:11
53.	2 Sam. 7:14a	The Son of God	Luke 1:32, Romans 1:3-4
54.	2 Sam. 7:16	David's house established forever	Luke 3:31; Rev. 22:16

#	Reference	Description	Fulfillment
55.	2 Ki. 2:11	The bodily ascension to heaven illustrated	Luke 24:51
56.	1 Chr. 17:11	David's Seed	Matthew 1:1, 9:27
57.	1 Chr. 17:12-13	To reign on David's throne forever	Luke 1:32, 33
58.	1 Chr. 17:13	"I will be His Father, He...my Son."	Hebrews 1:5
59.	Job 9:32-33	Mediator between man and God	1 Timothy 2:5
60.	Job 19:23-27	The Resurrection predicted	John 5:24-29
61.	Psa. 2:1-3	The enmity of kings foreordained	Acts 4:25-28
62.	Psa. 2:2	To own the title, Anointed (Christ)	John 1:41, Acts 2:36
63.	Psa. 2:6	His Character-Holiness	John 8:46; Revelation 3:7
64.	Psa. 2:6	To own the title King	Matthew 2:2
65.	Psa. 2:7	Declared the Beloved Son	Matthew 3:17, Romans 1:4
66.	Psa. 2:7, 8	The Crucifixion and Resurrection intimated	Acts 13:29-33
67.	Psa. 2:8, 9	Rule the nations with a rod of iron	Rev. 2:27, 12:5, 19:15
68.	Psa. 2:12	Life comes through faith in Him	John 20:31
69.	Psa. 8:2	The mouths of babes perfect His praise	Matthew 21:16
70.	Psa. 8:5, 6	His humiliation and exaltation	Hebrews 2:5-9
71.	Psa. 9:7-10	Judge the world in righteousness	Acts 17:31
72.	Psa. 16:10	Was not to see corruption	Acts 2:31, 13:35
73.	Psa. 16:9-11	Was to arise from the dead	John 20:9
74.	Psa. 17:15	The resurrection predicted	Luke 24:6
75.	Psa. 18:2-3	The horn of salvation	Luke 1:69-71

76.	Psa. 22:1	Forsaken because of sins of others	2 Corinthians 5:21
77.	Psa. 22:1	"My God, my God, why hast thou forsaken me?"	Matthew 27:46
78.	Psa. 22:2	Darkness upon Calvary for three hours	Matthew 27:45
79.	Psa. 22:7	They shoot out the lip and shake the head	Matthew 27:39-44
80.	Psa. 22:8	"He trusted in God, let Him deliver Him"	Matthew 27:43
81.	Psa. 22:9-10	Born the Saviour	Luke 2:7
82.	Psa. 22:12-13	They seek His death	John 19:6
83.	Psa. 22:14	His blood poured out when they pierced His side	John 19:34
84.	Psa. 22:14, 15	Suffered agony on Calvary	Mark 15:34-37
85.	Psa. 22:15	He thirsted	John 19:28
86.	Psa. 22:16	They pierced His hands and His feet	John 19:34, 37; 20:27
87.	Psa. 22:17, 18	Stripped Him before the stares of men	Luke 23:34, 35
88.	Psa. 22:18	They parted His garments	John 19:23, 24
89.	Psa. 22:20, 21	He committed Himself to God	Luke 23:46
90.	Psa. 22:20, 21	Satanic power bruising the Redeemer's heel	Hebrews 2:14
91.	Psa. 22:22	His Resurrection declared	John 20:17
92.	Psa. 22:27-28	He shall be the governor of the nations	Colossians 1:16
93.	Psa. 22:31	"It is finished"	John 19:30, Heb. 10:10, 12, 14, 18
94.	Psa. 23:1	"I am the Good Shepherd"	John 10:11, 1Peter 2:25
95.	Psa. 24:3	His exaltation predicted	Acts 1:11; Philippians 2:9
96.	Psa. 30:3	His resurrection predicted	Acts 2:32

97.	Psa. 31:5	"Into thy hands I commit my spirit"	Luke 23:46
98.	Psa. 31:11	His acquaintances fled from Him	Mark 14:50
99.	Psa. 31:13	They took counsel to put Him to death	Mt. 27:1, John 11:53
100.	Psa. 31:14, 15	"He trusted in God, let Him deliver him"	Matthew 27:43
101.	Psa. 34:20	Not a bone of Him broken	John 19:31-36
102.	Psa. 35:11	False witnesses rose up against Him	Matthew 26:59
103.	Psa. 35:19	He was hated without a cause	John 15:25
104.	Psa. 38:11	His friends stood afar off	Luke 23:49
105.	Psa. 38:12	Enemies try to entangle Him by craft	Mark 14:1, Mt. 22:15
106.	Psa. 38:12-13	Silent before His accusers	Matthew 27:12-14
107.	Psa. 38:20	He went about doing good	Acts 10:38
108.	Psa. 40:2-5	The joy of His resurrection predicted	John 20:20
109.	Psa. 40:6-8	His delight-the will of the Father	John 4:34, Heb. 10:5-10
110.	Psa. 40:9	He was to preach the Righteousness in Israel	Matthew 4:17
111.	Psa. 40:14	Confronted by adversaries in the Garden	John 18:4-6
112.	Psa. 41:9	Betrayed by a familiar friend	John 13:18
113.	Psa. 45:2	Words of Grace come from His lips	John 1:17, Luke 4:22
114.	Psa. 45:6	To own the title, God or Elohim	Hebrews 1:8
115.	Psa. 45:7	A special anointing by the Holy Spirit	Mt. 3:16; Heb. 1:9
116.	Psa. 45:7, 8	Called the Christ (Messiah or Anointed)	Luke 2:11

Crossing Over

117. Psa. 45:17	His name remembered forever	Ephesians 1:20-21, Heb. 1:8
118. Psa. 55:12-14	Betrayed by a friend, not an enemy	John 13:18
119. Psa. 55:15	Unrepentant death of the Betrayer	Matthew 27:3-5; Acts 1:16-19
120. Psa. 68:18	To give gifts to men	Ephesians 4:7-16
121. Psa. 68:18	Ascended into Heaven	Luke 24:51
122. Psa. 69:4	Hated without a cause	John 15:25
123. Psa. 69:8	A stranger to own brethren	John 1:11, 7:5
124. Psa. 69:9	Zealous for the Lord's House	John 2:17
125. Psa. 69:14-20	Messiah's anguish of soul before crucifixion	Matthew 26:36-45
126. Psa. 69:20	"My soul is exceeding sorrowful."	Matthew 26:38
127. Psa. 69:21	Given vinegar in thirst	Matthew 27:34
128. Psa. 69:26	The Saviour given and smitten by God	John 17:4; 18:11
129. Psa. 72:10, 11	Great persons were to visit Him	Matthew 2:1-11
130. Psa. 72:16	The corn of wheat to fall into the Ground	John 12:24-25
131. Psa. 72:17	Belief on His name will produce offspring	John 1:12, 13
132. Psa. 72:17	All nations shall be blessed by Him	Galatians 3:8
133. Psa. 72:17	All nations shall call Him blessed	John 12:13, Rev. 5:8-12
134. Psa. 78:1-2	He would teach in parables	Matthew 13:34-35
135. Psa. 78:2b	To speak the Wisdom of God with authority	Matthew 7:29
136. Psa. 80:17	The Man of God's right hand	Mark 14:61-62

137.	Psa. 88	The Suffering and Reproach of Calvary	Matthew 27:26-50
138.	Psa. 88:8	They stood afar off and watched	Luke 23:49
139.	Psa. 89:27	Firstborn	Colossians 1:15, 18
140.	Psa. 89:27	Emmanuel to be higher than earthly kings	Luke 1:32, 33
141.	Psa. 89:35-37	David's Seed, throne, kingdom endure forever	Luke 1:32, 33
142.	Psa. 89:36-37	His character-Faithfulness	Revelation 1:5, 19:11
143.	Psa. 90:2	He is from everlasting (Micah 5:2)	John 1:1
144.	Psa. 91:11, 12	Identified as Messianic; used to tempt Christ	Luke 4:10, 11
145.	Psa. 97:9	His exaltation predicted	Acts 1:11; Ephesians 1:20
146.	Psa. 100:5	His character-Goodness	Matthew 19:16, 17
147.	Psa. 102:1-11	The Suffering and Reproach of Calvary	John 19:16-30
148.	Psa. 102:25-27	Messiah is the Preexistent Son	Hebrews 1:10-12
149.	Psa. 109:25	Ridiculed	Matthew 27:39
150.	Psa. 110:1	Son of David	Matthew 22:42-43
151.	Psa. 110:1	To ascend to the right-hand of the Father	Mark 16:19
152.	Psa. 110:1	David's son called Lord	Matthew 22:44, 45
153.	Psa. 110:4	A priest after Melchizedek's order	Hebrews 6:20
154.	Psa. 112:4	His character-Compassionate, Gracious, et al	Matthew 9:36
155.	Psa. 118:17, 18	Messiah's Resurrection assured	Luke 24:5-7; 1Cor. 15:20
156.	Psa. 118:22, 23	The rejected stone is Head of the corner	Matthew 21:42, 43

#	Reference	Description	Fulfillment
157.	Psa. 118:26a	The Blessed One presented to Israel	Matthew 21:9
158.	Psa. 118:26b	To come while Temple standing	Matthew 21:12-15
159.	Psa. 132:11	The Seed of David (the fruit of His Body)	Luke 1:32, Act 2:30
160.	Psa. 129:3	He was scourged	Matthew 27:26
161.	Psa. 138:1-6	The supremacy of David's Seed amazes kings	Matthew 2:2-6
162.	Psa. 147:3, 6	The earthly ministry of Christ described	Luke 4:18
163.	Prov. 1:23	He will send the Spirit of God	John 16:7
164.	Prov. 8:23	Foreordained from everlasting	Rev. 13:8, 1Peter 1:19-20
165.	Song. 5:16	The altogether lovely One	John 1:17
166.	Isa. 2:3	He shall teach all nations	John 4:25
167.	Isa. 2:4	He shall judge among the nations	John 5:22
168.	Isa. 6:1	When Isaiah saw His glory	John 12:40-41
169.	Isa. 6:8	The One Sent by God	John 12:38-45
170.	Isa. 6:9-10	Parables fall on deaf ears	Matthew 13:13-15
171.	Isa. 6:9-12	Blinded to Christ and deaf to His words	Acts 28:23-29
172.	Isa. 7:14	To be born of a virgin	Luke 1:35
173.	Isa. 7:14	To be Emmanuel-God with us	Matthew 1:18-23, 1Tim. 3:16
174.	Isa. 8:8	Called Emmanuel	Matthew 28:20
175.	Isa. 8:14	A stone of stumbling, a Rock of offense	1Peter 2:8
176.	Isa. 9:1, 2	His ministry to begin in Galilee	Matthew 4:12-17
177.	Isa. 9:6	A child born-Humanity	Luke 1:31
178.	Isa. 9:6	A Son given-Deity	Luke 1:32, John 1:14, 1Tim. 3:16

#	Verse	Description	Reference
179.	Isa. 9:6	Declared to be the Son of God with power	Romans 1:3, 4
180.	Isa. 9:6	The Wonderful One, Peleh	Luke 4:22
181.	Isa. 9:6	The Counsellor, Yaatz	Matthew 13:54
182.	Isa. 9:6	The Mighty God, El Gibor	1Cor. 1:24, Titus 2:13
183.	Isa. 9:6	The Everlasting Father, Avi Adth	John 8:58, 10:30
184.	Isa. 9:6	The Prince of Peace, Sar Shalom	John 16:33
185.	Isa. 9:7	Inherits the throne of David	Luke 1:32
186.	Isa. 9:7	His Character-Just	John 5:30
187.	Isa. 9:7	No end to his Government, Throne, and kingdom	Luke 1:33
188.	Isa. 11:1	Called a Nazarene-the Branch, Netzer	Matthew 2:23
189.	Isa. 11:1	A rod out of Jesse-Son of Jesse	Luke 3:23, 32
190.	Isa. 11:2	Anointed One by the Spirit	Matthew 3:16, 17, Acts 10:38
191.	Isa. 11:2	His Character-Wisdom, Knowledge, et al	Colossians 2:3
192.	Isa. 11:3	He would know their thoughts	Luke 6:8, John 2:25
193.	Isa. 11:4	Judge in righteousness	Acts 17:31
194.	Isa. 11:4	Judges with the sword of His mouth	Rev. 2:16, 19:11, 15
195.	Isa. 11:5	Character: Righteous & Faithful	Rev. 19:11
196.	Isa. 11:10	The Gentiles seek Him	John 12:18-21
197.	Isa. 12:2	Called Jesus-Yeshua	Matthew 1:21
198.	Isa. 22:22	The One given all authority to govern	Revelation 3:7
199.	Isa. 25:8	The Resurrection predicted	1Corinthians 15:54

200. Isa. 26:19	His power of Resurrection predicted	Matthew 27:50-54
201. Isa. 28:16	The Messiah is the precious corner stone	Acts 4:11, 12
202. Isa. 28:16	The Sure Foundation	1Corinthians 3:11, Mt. 16:18
203. Isa. 29:13	He indicated hypocritical obedience to His Word	Matthew 15:7-9
204. Isa. 29:14	The wise are confounded by the Word	1Corinthians 1:18-31
205. Isa. 32:2	A Refuge-A man shall be a hiding place	Matthew 23:37
206. Isa. 35:4	He will come and save you	Matthew 1:21
207. Isa. 35:5-6	To have a ministry of miracles	Matthew 11:2-6
208. Isa. 40:3, 4	Preceded by forerunner	John 1:23
209. Isa. 40:9	"Behold your God."	John 1:36; 19:14
210. Isa. 40:10.	He will come to reward	Revelation 22:12
211. Isa. 40:11	A shepherd-compassionate life-giver	John 10:10-18
212. Isa. 42:1-4	The Servant-as a faithful, patient redeemer	Matthew 12:18-21
213. Isa. 42:2	Meek and lowly	Matthew 11:28-30
214. Isa. 42:3	He brings hope for the hopeless	John 4
215. Isa. 42:4	The nations shall wait on His teachings	John 12:20-26
216. Isa. 42:6	The Light (salvation) of the Gentiles	Luke 2:32
217. Isa. 42:1, 6	His is a worldwide compassion	Matthew 28:19, 20
218. Isa. 42:7	Blind eyes opened.	John 9:25-38
219. Isa. 43:11	He is the only Saviour.	Acts 4:12
220. Isa. 44:3	He will send the Spirit of God	John 16:7, 13

#	Reference	Description	Fulfillment
221.	Isa. 45:21-25	He is Lord and Saviour	Philippians 3:20, Titus 2:13
222.	Isa. 45:23	He will be the Judge	John 5:22; Romans 14:11
223.	Isa. 46:9, 10	Declares things not yet done	John 13:19
224.	Isa. 48:12	The First and the Last	John 1:30, Revelation 1:8, 17
225.	Isa. 48:16, 17	He came as a Teacher	John 3:2
226.	Isa. 49:1	Called from the womb-His humanity	Matthew 1:18
227.	Isa. 49:5	A Servant from the womb.	Luke 1:31, Philippians 2:7
228.	Isa. 49:6	He will restore Israel	Acts 3:19-21, 15:16-17
229.	Isa. 49:6	He is Salvation for Israel	Luke 2:29-32
230.	Isa. 49:6	He is the Light of the Gentiles	John 8:12, Acts 13:47
231.	Isa. 49:6	He is Salvation unto the ends of the earth	Acts 15:7-18
232.	Isa. 49:7	He is despised of the Nation	John 1:11, 8:48-49, 19:14-15
233.	Isa. 50:3	Heaven is clothed in black at His humiliation	Luke 23:44, 45
234.	Isa. 50:4	He is a learned counselor for the weary	Matthew 7:29, 11:28, 29
235.	Isa. 50:5	The Servant bound willingly to obedience	Matthew 26:39
236.	Isa. 50:6a	"I gave my back to the smiters."	Matthew 27:26
237.	Isa. 50:6b	He was smitten on the cheeks	Matthew 26:67
238.	Isa. 50:6c	He was spat upon	Matthew 27:30
239.	Isa. 52:7	Published good tidings upon mountains	Matthew 5:12,15:29,28:16
240.	Isa. 52:13	The Servant exalted	Acts 1:8-11; Eph. 1:19-22, Php. 2:5-9

#	Reference	Description	Fulfillment
241.	Isa. 52:14	The Servant shockingly abused	Luke 18:31-34; Mt. 26:67, 68
242.	Isa. 52:15	Nations startled by message of the Servant	Luke 18:31-34; Mt. 26:67, 68
243.	Isa. 52:15	His blood shed sprinkles nations	Hebrews 9:13-14, Rev. 1:5
244.	Isa. 53:1	His people would not believe Him	John 12:37-38
245.	Isa. 53:2	Appearance of an ordinary man	Philippians 2:6-8
246.	Isa. 53:3a	Despised	Luke 4:28-29
247.	Isa. 53:3b	Rejected	Matthew 27:21-23
248.	Isa. 53:3c	Great sorrow and grief	Matthew 26:37-38, Luke 19:41, Heb. 4:15
249.	Isa. 53:3d	Men hide from being associated with Him	Mark 14:50-52
250.	Isa. 53:4a	He would have a healing ministry	Matthew 8:16-17
251.	Isa. 53:4b	Thought to be cursed by God	Matthew 26:66, 27:41-43
252.	Isa. 53:5a	Bears penalty for mankind's iniquities	2Cor. 5:21, Heb. 2:9
253.	Isa. 53:5b	His sacrifice provides peace between man and God	Colossians 1:20
254.	Isa. 53:5c	His sacrifice would heal man of sin	1Peter 2:24
255.	Isa. 53:6a	He would be the sin-bearer for all mankind	1John 2:2, 4:10
256.	Isa. 53:6b	God's will that He bear sin for all mankind	Galatians 1:4
257.	Isa. 53:7a	Oppressed and afflicted	Matthew 27:27-31
258.	Isa. 53:7b	Silent before his accusers	Matthew 27:12-14
259.	Isa. 53:7c	Sacrificial lamb	John 1:29, 1Peter 1:18-19
260.	Isa. 53:8a	Confined and persecuted	Matthew 26:47-27:31

#	Verse	Description	Reference
261.	Isa. 53:8b	He would be judged	John 18:13-22
262.	Isa. 53:8c	Killed	Matthew 27:35
263.	Isa. 53:8d	Dies for the sins of the world	1John 2:2
264.	Isa. 53:9a	Buried in a rich man's grave	Matthew 27:57
265.	Isa. 53:9b	Innocent and had done no violence	Luke 23:41, John 18:38
266.	Isa. 53:9c	No deceit in his mouth	1Peter 2:22
267.	Isa. 53:10a	God's will that He die for mankind	John 18:11
268.	Isa. 53:10b	An offering for sin	Matthew 20:28, Galatians 3:13
269.	Isa. 53:10c	Resurrected and live forever	Romans 6:9
270.	Isa. 53:10d	He would prosper	John 17:1-5
271.	Isa. 53:11a	God fully satisfied with His suffering	John 12:27
272.	Isa. 53:11b	God's servant would justify man	Romans 5:8-9, 18-19
273.	Isa. 53:11c	The sin-bearer for all mankind	Hebrews 9:28
274.	Isa. 53:12a	Exalted by God because of his sacrifice	Matthew 28:18
275.	Isa. 53:12b	He would give up his life to save mankind	Luke 23:46
276.	Isa. 53:12c	Numbered with the transgressors	Mark 15:27-28
277.	Isa. 53:12d	Sin-bearer for all mankind	1Peter 2:24
278.	Isa. 53:12e	Intercede to God in behalf of mankind	Luke 23:34, Rom. 8:34
279.	Isa. 55:3	Resurrected by God	Acts 13:34
280.	Isa. 55:4a	A witness	John 18:37
281.	Isa. 55:4b	He is a leader and commander	Hebrews 2:10
282.	Isa. 55:5	God would glorify Him	Acts 3:13

#	Reference	Description	Fulfillment
283.	Isa. 59:16a	Intercessor between man and God	Matthew 10:32
284.	Isa. 59:16b	He would come to provide salvation	John 6:40
285.	Isa. 59:20	He would come to Zion as their Redeemer	Luke 2:38
286.	Isa. 60:1-3	He would shew light to the Gentiles	Acts 26:23
287.	Isa. 61:1a	The Spirit of God upon him	Matthew 3:16-17
288.	Isa. 61:1b	The Messiah would preach the good news	Luke 4:16-21
289.	Isa. 61:1c	Provide freedom from the bondage of sin	John 8:31-36
290.	Isa. 61:1-2a	Proclaim a period of grace	Galatians 4:4-5
291.	Jer. 11:21	Conspiracy to kill Jesus	John 7:1, Matthew 21:38
292.	Jer. 23:5-6	Descendant of David	Luke 3:23-31
293.	Jer. 23:5-6	The Messiah would be both God and Man	John 13:13, 1Ti 3:16
294.	Jer. 31:22	Born of a virgin	Matthew 1:18-20
295.	Jer. 31:31	The Messiah would be the new covenant	Matthew 26:28
296.	Jer. 33:14-15	Descendant of David	Luke 3:23-31
297.	Eze.34:23-24	Descendant of David	Matthew 1:1
298.	Eze.37:24-25	Descendant of David	Luke 1:31-33
299.	Dan. 2:44-45	The Stone that shall break the kingdoms	Matthew 21:44
300.	Dan. 7:13-14a	He would ascend into heaven	Acts 1:9-11
301.	Dan. 7:13-14b	Highly exalted	Ephesians 1:20-22
302.	Dan. 7:13-14c	His dominion would be everlasting	Luke 1:31-33

#	Reference	Description	Fulfillment
303.	Dan. 9:24a	To make an end to sins	Galatians 1:3-5
304.	Dan. 9:24a	To make reconciliation for iniquity	Romans 5:10, 2Cor. 5:18-21
305.	Dan. 9:24b	He would be holy	Luke 1:35
306.	Dan. 9:25	His announcement	John 12:12-13
307.	Dan. 9:26a	Cut off	Matthew 16:21, 21:38-39
308.	Dan. 9:26b	Die for the sins of the world	Hebrews 2:9
309.	Dan. 9:26c	Killed before the destruction of the temple	Matthew 27:50-51
310.	Dan. 10:5-6	Messiah in a glorified state	Revelation 1:13-16
311.	Hos. 11:1	He would be called out of Egypt	Matthew 2:15
312.	Hos. 13:14	He would defeat death	1Corinthians 15:55-57
313.	Joel 2:32	Offer salvation to all mankind	Romans 10:9-13
314.	Jonah 1:17	Death and resurrection of Christ	Matthew 12:40, 16:4
315.	Mic. 5:2a	Born in Bethlehem	Matthew 2:1-6
316.	Mic. 5:2b	Ruler in Israel	Luke 1:33
317.	Mic. 5:2c	From everlasting	John 8:58
318.	Hag. 2:6-9	He would visit the second Temple	Luke 2:27-32
319.	Hag. 2:23	Descendant of Zerubbabel	Luke 2:27-32
320.	Zech. 3:8	God's servant	John 17:4
321.	Zech. 6:12-13	Priest and King	Hebrews 8:1
322.	Zech. 9:9a	Greeted with rejoicing in Jerusalem	Matthew 21:8-10
323.	Zech. 9:9b	Beheld as King	John 12:12-13
324.	Zech. 9:9c	The Messiah would be just	John 5:30
325.	Zech. 9:9d	The Messiah would bring salvation	Luke 19:10

#	Reference	Description	Fulfillment
326.	Zech. 9:9e	The Messiah would be humble	Matthew 11:29
327.	Zech. 9:9f	Presented to Jerusalem riding on a donkey	Matthew 21:6-9
328.	Zech. 10:4	The cornerstone	Ephesians 2:20
329.	Zech. 11:4-6a	At His coming, Israel to have unfit leaders	Matthew 23:1-4
330.	Zech. 11:4-6b	Rejection causes God to remove His protection	Luke 19:41-44
331.	Zech. 11:4-6c	Rejected in favor of another king	John 19:13-15
332.	Zech. 11:7	Ministry to "poor," the believing remnant	Matthew 9:35-36
333.	Zech. 11:8a	Unbelief forces Messiah to reject them	Matthew 23:33
334.	Zech. 11:8b	Despised	Matthew 27:20
335.	Zech. 11:9	Stops ministering to those who rejected Him	Matthew 13:10-11
336.	Zech. 11:10-11a	Rejection causes God to remove protection	Luke 19:41-44
337.	Zech. 11:10-11b	The Messiah would be God	John 14:7
338.	Zech. 11:12-13a	Betrayed for thirty pieces of silver	Matthew 26:14-15
339.	Zech. 11:12-13b	Rejected	Matthew 26:14-15
340.	Zech. 11:12-13c	Thirty pieces of silver cast in the house of the Lord	Matthew 27:3-5
341.	Zech. 11:12-13d	The Messiah would be God	John 12:45
342.	Zech. 12:10a	The Messiah's body would be pierced	John 19:34-37
343.	Zech. 12:10b	The Messiah would be both God and man	John 10:30
344.	Zech. 12:10c	The Messiah would be rejected	John 1:11

345.	Zech. 13:7a	God's will He die for mankind	John 18:11
346.	Zech. 13:7b	A violent death	Mark 14:27
347.	Zech. 13:7c	Both God and man	John 14:9
348.	Zech. 13:7d	Israel scattered as a result of rejecting Him	Matthew 26:31-56
349.	Zech. 14:4	He would return to the Mt. of Olives	Acts 1:11-12
350.	Mal. 3:1a	Messenger to prepare the way for Messiah	Mark 1:1-8
351.	Mal. 3:1b	Sudden appearance at the temple	Mark 11:15-16
352.	Mal. 3:1c	Messenger of the new covenant	Luke 4:43
353.	Mal. 3:6	The God who changes not	Hebrews 13:8
354.	Mal. 4:5	Forerunner in spirit of Elijah	Mt. 3:1-3, 11:10-14, 17:11-13
355.	Mal. 4:6	Forerunner would turn many to righteousness	Luke 1:16-17

ABOUT THE AUTHOR

Jay Rice is a deep Biblical researcher holding a Certificate of Biblical Studies in Bible Languages and Hebraic Roots and Theology from International School of the Word. He is also a student at the American Institute College. By searching out the deep things of God, Jay has dug deep into our Hebraic Roots to tell us what God has shown him. He has learned the deeper you go into the Word of God the deeper God will take you, showing you great & mighty things that you may not know of!